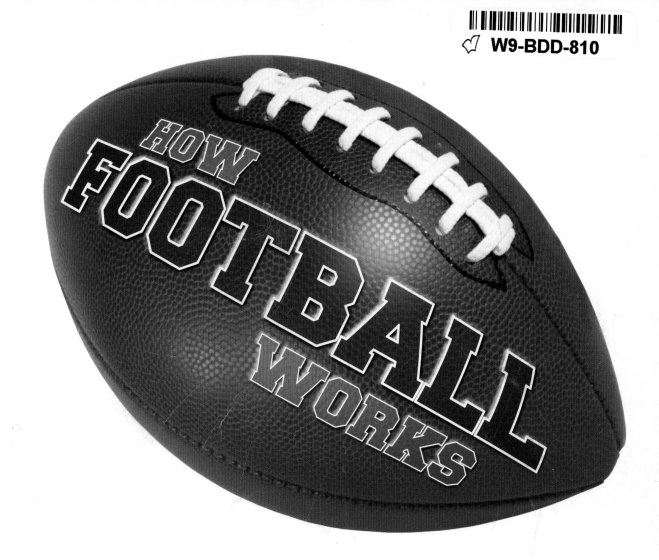

HOW FOOTBALL WORKS

Keltie Thomas

Illustrations by Stephen MacEachern

MAPLE
TREE
PRESS

Maple Tree books are published by Owlkids Books Inc.
10 Lower Spadina Avenue, Suite 400, Toronto, Ontario M5V 2Z2
www.owlkids.com

Text © 2010 Keltie Thomas
Illustrations © 2010 Stephen MacEachern

Distributed in Canada by Raincoast Books
9050 Shaughnessy Street, Vancouver, British Columbia V6P 6E5

Distributed in the United States by Publishers Group West
1700 Fourth Street, Berkeley, California 94710

Dedication
For football fans everywhere

Acknowledgments
Many thanks to all the wonderful people at Maple Tree and Owlkids,
especially Anne Shone, without whom this book could not have been written,
Stephen MacEachern, Ted Darling, Laura Stanley, Roger Yip, Ajax Pickering Dolphins
Football Club, Margaret Eskins, Holly Eskins, Taylor Eskins, Suzie Brown,
Delante Brown, Sarah Higgins, Katey Higgins, Robert Leduc, and Brian Findlay.

Library and Archives Canada Cataloguing in Publication
Thomas, Keltie
How football works / Keltie Thomas ; illustrated by Stephen MacEachern.

(How sports work)
Includes index.
ISBN 978-1-897349-87-8 (bound).--ISBN 978-1-897349-88-5 (pbk.)

1. Football--Juvenile literature. I. MacEachern, Stephen II. Title.
III. Series: How sports work

GV950.7.T56 2010   j796.332   C2010-900557-0

Library of Congress Control Number: 2010920481

Design and illustration: Stephen MacEachern   Photo Credits: see page 64

Canada Council   Conseil des Arts
for the Arts   du Canada

ONTARIO ARTS COUNCIL
CONSEIL DES ARTS DE L'ONTARIO

We acknowledge the financial support of the Canada Council for the Arts, the Ontario
Arts Council, the Government of Canada through the Canada Book Fund (CBF),
and the Government of Ontario through the Ontario Media Development
Corporation's Book Initiative for our publishing activities.

Manufactured by Print Plus Limited
Manufactured in Guangdong, China in July 2010
Job #S100700379

A   B   C   D   E   F

CONTENTS

4 How Does Football Work?
6 Legends of the Game
   Football: Born in the U.S.A.

Chapter 1

7   That's the Way the Ball Bounces
12 Legends of the Game
    Totally Sick Hidden Ball Trick

Chapter 2

13 The Players
20 Legends of the Game
    The Fridge Freezes the Opposition

Chapter 3

21 The Field
28 Legends of the Game
    The Ice Bowl Rocks the Game

Chapter 4

29 **The Complete Athlete**

36 **Legends of the Game**
Brees and the Saints Go Marching In

Chapter 5

37 **Preparing for Battle**

44 **Legends of the Game**
How the Giants Outsmarted
the Bears

Chapter 6

45 **The Science of Explosive Moves**

52 **Legends of the Game**
The Ball Takes Flight

Chapter 7

53 **Game Time**

60 **Rules & Regs**

62 **Football Talk**

64 **Index**

HOW DOES FOOTBALL WORK?

Fans, players, and inquiring minds everywhere want to know!

What makes football the most strategic game on Earth? What makes the ball bounce and roll so unpredictably? Why do kickers get their very own ball? How do teams prepare for battle? How do ground crews get the field in tip-top shape? Why are helmets football players' most important piece of equipment? What makes a tackle such a big hit? How do the rules of the game differ between the NFL (National Football League) and the CFL (Canadian Football League)? And what's the score on touchdowns and field goals?

Well, just like everything else on Earth, it all comes down to science (plus a few things science hasn't managed to explain yet!). And if you think that makes football sound boring, you'd better check out what planet you're on. But, hey, why don't you turn the page and check out the world of football in action for yourself?

Whether you want answers to those burning questions, tips on becoming a better player, the scoop on inside information, or just to have a blast with the game, this book's for you.

Hey! You don't have to be a football maniac to read this book. The Rules and Regs and Football Talk are decoded on pages 60 and 62.

Harvard University
Football Club, 1875

Football: Born in the U.S.A.

Forget soccer! Forget rugby! Let's invent a new game. That's what a bunch of Boston schoolboys did in the 1860s. Bored out of their skulls with the two games, the boys combined kicking from soccer and running with the ball from rugby to create the "Boston Game."

As the boys grew up, some went to Harvard University and brought the Boston Game with them. But no other U.S. school played it. So Harvard looked to McGill University in Montreal, Canada, where students played traditional rugby. The schools challenged each other to a couple of games: one played with Harvard's Boston rules and the other played with McGill's rugby rules.

The two games were very different and even used different balls. Harvard played with a round ball whereas McGill used a rugby ball that was twice as big and shaped like an egg. Harvard won the game played with their rules easily. But to everyone's surprise, Harvard held McGill to a scoreless tie in the game played with McGill's rugby rules.

Harvard took up the weird egg-shaped ball, and soon challenged Yale University to a rugby game. And even though Harvard trounced Yale, Yale fell in love with the sport and began playing it themselves.

The game spread to other U.S. schools and the schools began tinkering with the rules. Some elements of rugby were dropped, and some elements were invented on the spot, until a whole new game came to be. And so the sport of football bounced into the world on American soil.

Chapter 1

THAT'S THE WAY THE BALL BOUNCES

Whomp! Zoom! A kicker boots the ball toward the end zone as the clock counts down the game's final seconds. Fans hold their breath. Will the kick send the ball through the goal posts for a field goal? Or will it veer off target, dashing all hope of victory? *Boing!*

Pffffftt! A quarterback hurls the ball. Will the ball find an open receiver? Will the receiver carry the ball into the opponents' end zone for a touchdown? Or will the ball slip through his fingers?

Even though more than half of the players in a football game never touch the ball, the ball is always at the heart of the action. Players snap it, throw it, catch it, kick it, run with it, fight for it, and jump on opponents who have it. Find out what makes the ball bounce unpredictably and how it has put the *oomph* in the game through time.

Bounce this Way! ≫

BALL WITH PERSONALITY

Quick Hit

In the U.S., women play football with exactly the same rules as men. The only difference is that they use a smaller ball.

What makes this oddball a tough character to throw and kick around?

IT WEARS A LEATHER JACKET.

The official NFL ball sports a brown leather jacket. The jacket is made of four panels of cowhide. Tons of tiny round bumps called pebbles cover the entire surface. These pebbles make the ball feel rough and grainy rather than smooth and slippery, which helps players grip the ball. According to the official rules of the game, the jacket must not have wrinkles or folds of any kind. After all, it's the rulemakers' job to iron out any kinks of the game.

IT'S A FUNNY SHAPE.

Baseballs, tennis balls, soccer balls, golf balls, volleyballs, beach balls, and even gumballs are all perfectly round. But not a football. Oh, no! A football is shaped like an egg. It's fat and round in the middle and thin and pointy at both ends. But unlike an egg, both ends of a football are exactly the same. This funny shape makes the ball difficult to handle and kick. It also makes the ball bounce and roll unpredictably. When the ball hits the ground, it might bounce forward, backward, or even roll over the ground before it bounces. Talk about a total oddball!

IT'S GOT LACES.

The ball has eight white laces across the center of its belly. Not only do these laces sew up the ball and hold it together, but they also help players get a grip. The laces stick out from the ball, giving players something to hold on to. In fact, quarterbacks wrap their pinky finger, fourth finger, and middle finger in between the laces for a good grip. Some college and high school teams have even used balls with pebbled laces that feel grainy, like the ball's jacket, to get a better grip on the ball.

IT'S BROKEN IN.

Ever seen a shoe buffer machine? The NFL uses a machine like it to break in official game balls so that each one feels and handles the same way. It does the job faster and more effectively than rubbing the ball by hand, and more reliably than any team. The NFL began breaking in balls after the 1996 Super Bowl, when the Pittsburgh Steelers and Dallas Cowboys argued over how the job was done. Before that, some teams secretly doctored the ball to alter its performance. The sly teams cooked the ball, put it in a dryer, filled it with helium gas rather than air, and even rubbed it with oil.

IT STAYS IN SHAPE.

The size and weight of the ball affect how it flies through the air, so all NFL balls get measured and weighed to ensure they're fit to play. The official NFL rules say the ball must be 28 to 28.5 cm (11 to 11 ¼ in.) long, 53 to 54 cm (21 to 21 ¼ in.) around the belly, or middle, and weigh in at 400 to 425 g (14 to 15 oz.). What's more, the ball is filled with 5.7 to 6 kg (12 ½ to 13 ½ lbs.) of air pressure to help it hold its shape as players squeeze it, grab it, pound it, and kick it.

TIP

Not quite the same size as the average pro? Play with a kid-sized football to complete your passes, kicks, and catches.

Get Under Its Skin

Here's how pro balls are put together inside and out. First, factory workers press and stamp cowhide with machines to create the pebble-grain finish of the ball's outer jacket. A worker then uses a cookie cutter-like tool to cut panels out of the cowhide. A vinyl-cotton lining is then sewn onto each panel to give the ball the strength to hold its shape even through kicking and pounding by 135-kg (300-lb.) linemen. Next, a sewing machine operator sews four panels together inside out. A worker then steams the panels and uses a machine to punch, or break, the ends. This softens the panels so they can be turned right-side out. Then a polyurethane bladder is inserted and filled with air. A worker then laces up the ball and puts it into a mold for final shaping. Once it pops out, the ball's ready to ship to the NFL.

Polyurethane bladder

Vinyl-cotton lining

Cowhide

IT'S MARKED.

Pssst. The ball is marked for life or else it doesn't get into the game. Also, it must be handpicked and stamped with the signature of the NFL commissioner. Before every game, the referee unpacks twelve new balls specially marked with a "K" and sets them aside to be used only for kicking plays. That's not all: balls made especially for the Super Bowl get marked with a synthetic DNA. Just like DNA, which carries hereditary information, can identify people, the synthetic DNA identifies the official balls. The DNA marker glows under laser light. That way, people can tell real Super Bowl balls, which sell for big bucks, from fakes.

SPIRALING THROUGH TIME

Quick Hit

A yard equals 3 ft. (.9144 m). That's just a bit longer than three footballs placed end to end. Even in Canada, where the metric system of measurement is used, football gains are talked about in yards.

Check out how the football got its funny shape and how it has shaped the game through time.

2000 BCE

The oldest-known balls roll into the world fashioned out of wood, leather, and papyrus by the ancient Egyptians.

2000–800 BCE

Ancient Greeks make a ball out of a pig's bladder, wrapped in pigskin. Men and women battle for the ball in a game called *Episkyros*. Greek scholar Julius Pollux describes players faking each other out by "showing the ball to one man and then throwing it to another."

146 BCE

The Romans conquer Greece and soon make the game their own. They add kicking, give the game a new name—*Harpastum*—and use a smaller ball made of leather and stuffed with sponges or animal fur. What's more, the Romans allow tackling.

1869

Rutgers and Princeton play what's called "the first college football game." But they play the game of soccer and use a round ball to boot.

1874

Harvard University picks up a love for rugby and the odd oval-shaped rugby ball in a series of games against McGill University (see page 6).

1876

Harvard combines soccer and rugby rules with the funny-shaped rugby ball and introduces them to Yale University. Several U.S. colleges take up the game—and football is born!

1880

When the ball goes out of bounds, opponents shove each other, fighting for it. Instead, rulemaker Walter Camp suggests an offensive player put the ball in play by snapping it back to his quarterback. This allows the team that had the ball to keep it. Since gaining possession of the ball is no longer left to chance, teams begin to plan maneuvers.

1882

With the snap rule (see above) comes trouble as it allows teams to keep the ball for an entire game. Camp solves the problem with a new rule that requires teams to gain 5 yards in three plays, or downs, or give up the ball.

1888

Carrying the ball becomes a tough job as a new rule allows players to tackle, or hit, opponents below the waist and above the knees.

1896

A ball that looks like a stretched-out pumpkin replaces the rugby ball. An official description of the ball mentions only its shape—a prolate spheroid—or imperfect sphere lengthened at the ends.

1905

Wham! Bam! Players collide and often pile up in a huge heavy heap. The bone-crushing collisions cause serious injuries and kill eighteen players. Many people demand the game be banned. So the next year, passing the ball forward becomes legal as rulemakers try to clean up the brutal violence. They also increase the distance teams must gain in three downs from 5 to 10 yards.

1930

The ball gets a makeover. It's made slimmer at the middle and more pointed at the ends to improve passing.

1999

Whomp! ...and another kickoff reaches the end zone. The NFL suspects that kickers are doctoring the ball to make it fly farther. Rumor has it they are doing everything from taking a power-sander to the ball to microwaving it, to wiping it down with milk. The NFL decides that kickers must use a new ball that gets only a brief rubdown by the team equipment handler. And so the K ball (see page 9) enters the game and the number of returns drops.

Quick Hit

NFL and CFL rules call for slightly different-sized balls. What's more, CFL balls sport a white stripe around each end while NFL balls have no stripes at all.

2007

With his team just a field goal away from victory, quarterback Tony Romo (above) holds the ball in place for the kicker and the ball slips out of his grasp. The fumble costs the Dallas Cowboys a playoff spot. Everyone blames the K ball for being slippery. And maybe the NFL bigwigs agree as they decide that equipment handlers can have more than twice as much time to rub down K balls before games.

Beyond

Making a ball that feels perfect in players' hands right out of the box, and stays that way, is the ultimate goal for ballmakers. Future balls may wear synthetic jackets that don't soak up as much rain or harden up as much in cold weather.

What's football?

You know it as a game played with a funny-shaped ball on a field shaped like a shoebox. But outside of North America, the name "football" almost always refers to the game of soccer. And in Australia, it refers to a game played with a rugby-like ball on an oval-shaped field.

What's "the pigskin"?

A nickname for the ball. Although the ball may feel like tough pigskin, it's actually made of cowhide (see page 9). However, some early soccer and rugby balls were made of inflated pigs' bladders.

Do officials keep tabs on the K ball?

You bet! The night before an NFL game, a sealed box of K balls is delivered to the officials' hotel. An official checks that the seal has not been broken and doesn't let the box out of his sight until he takes it to the stadium the next day. He even sleeps in the same room as the box!

Carlisle Indians

Totally Sick Hidden Ball Trick

Say your team is on defense. Your placekicker boots the ball downfield to your opponents and *poof*—the ball disappears completely. The Crimson of Harvard faced this situation against the Carlisle Indians in 1903. After receiving the kick, all the Carlisle players rushed toward the Crimson players, each one hugging his stomach as if *he* had the ball. The Crimson players looked around wildly. But the ball was nowhere in sight.

The Harvard fans burst into laughter in the stands once they figured out who had the ball, while the Crimson players remained clueless. Seconds later, the Indians' lineman, Charlie Dillon, zoomed over the Harvard end line. The Indians' quarterback, Jimmie Johnson, then grabbed the ball out of Dillon's jersey and slammed it on the turf. Touchdown! Harvard couldn't believe it. How had Dillon managed to sprint 103 yards with the ball right under their noses?

On the kickoff, Dillon and Johnson had dropped back behind a wall of their teammates. Johnson caught the ball and stuffed it into the back of Dillon's jersey, which had an elastic waistband specially sewn in for the trick. Then the Indians took off in all directions. Harvard protested, but there were no rules against the play, so the touchdown stood. This trick was eventually outlawed, but not before becoming one of the most spectacular plays in football history.

Chapter 2

THE PLAYERS

Sixty minutes or bust! In the early days of football, playing for the full hour was players' "code of conduct." The players didn't leave the field for the entire game unless they got injured. When their team lost possession of the ball, the players just switched from offense to defense and kept right on going—blocking, tackling, running, and hitting to their heart's desire. *Bam!*

But nowadays, pro teams have a different set of players for offense and defense and even special teams for kickoffs, kick returns, and other critical plays. So when teams change possession of the ball, they also change their onfield lineup. The offense or defense file off to the bench and their counterparts march on raring to go. Get the skinny on who's who on the field, what each position does, and how opponents line up in each other's faces to match wits.

Green Bay Packers'
Ryan Grant

Charge Ahead! ➤

WHO'S WHO?

Quick Hit

If it's "third and eight," that means it's third down with 8 yards needed to get a first down.

When two NFL teams duel on the gridiron, they each bring eleven players. That's twenty-two players, and each one has a different job. Check out this guide to who's who on the field, and match the numbers to the art to see who does what.

THE OFFENSE

The Offensive Line

Five big, agile players make up the offensive line: a center, flanked by two guards, and two tackles outside the guards.

❶ The Center

The center snaps the ball between his legs to the quarterback, calls signals for the line, and coordinates the linemen to block—run interference for a running play or pass. A player blocks an opponent by making contact with the opponent and using his hands, arms, and shoulders to move the opponent aside.

❷ The Guards

Powerful. That's what guards are. The guards push and shove defensive linemen to open up running lanes for their teammate carrying the ball. They also fend off defensive tackles, the biggest players on the field.

❸ The Tackles

It sounds crazy but offensive tackles cannot tackle without getting a penalty. Their job is to stop defenders without wrapping their arms around the defenders or grabbing on.

TIP

The numbers on NFL jerseys can help you tell the positions players play:
- Quarterbacks and kickers wear 1 to 19.
- Running backs and defensive backs wear 20 to 49.
- Offensive linemen wear 50 to 79.
- Linebackers wear 50 to 59 or 90 to 99.
- Defensive linemen wear 60 to 79 or 90 to 99.
- Receivers and tight ends wear 80 to 89.

❹ The Quarterback

He leads the team, calls plays, throws passes, runs with the ball, and reads the defense to figure out what they're up to. The quarterback has the biggest, most glamorous, and dangerous job on the field. But, hey, somebody's got to do it.

❺ The Running Backs

These players take the ball from the quarterback and light out for the goal line. Often one running back, called a fullback, clears the way for another, called a halfback, who carries the ball.

❻ The Tight End

This player lines up next to one of the offensive tackles. Not only does he receive passes, but he also blocks opponents. So he is usually bigger and stronger than other receivers and adds blocking power to the offensive line. What's more, the side of the line where the tight end sets up is called the strong side. And the defense often sets up to counter it.

❼ The Wide Receivers

Clear it out! Wide receivers line up to the right or left away from the offensive line. They block on running plays. But their main job is to zoom down the field, get open to catch the football, and run with it to the opponent's end zone. Even if they don't get open, they lure defensive players on their tail, clearing out an area for a shorter pass or running play.

THE OFFENSE

THE DEFENSE

The Defensive Line

Four, or sometimes three, big, agile, and strong linemen called tackles and ends make up the defensive line.

❽ The Tackles

One or two tackles set up in the middle of the defensive line. If it's one, this player is called a nose tackle because he lines up nose to nose with the center of the offensive line. Tackles are bigger linemen than the ends of the defensive line. Their job is to tie up opponents, and catch any and all ball carriers who come within reach.

❾ The Ends

These defensive linemen are usually smaller and quicker than tackles. Their job is to break through the offensive line, creating holes for other defenders to come through to hit the ball carrier or the quarterback. And if they get a chance to make a hit themselves, they'll take it. *Bam!*

❿ The Linebackers

Lining up a few yards behind the defensive line, linebackers are backup for the linemen. They stop running plays, rush and sack the quarterback, and help cover passing plays.

⓫ The Middle Linebacker

Say hello to the quarterback of the defense. In the huddle, the middle linebacker calls the plays for the defense. And once the huddle breaks, he scans the field and yells out what he sees. For example, he may yell "Strength right" to tell his teammates that the tight end is lined up on the right side of the offensive line.

The Secondary

As if backup from the linebackers wasn't enough, the defense also has a secondary of four defensive backs: two cornerbacks and two safeties.

⓬ The Cornerbacks

These players cover and tackle wide receivers. Their job is to stop receivers from catching the ball.

⓭ The Safeties

Meet the last line of defense. The safeties help out where needed. The "strong safety" plays on the same side as the tight end to cover any passes to the tight end. He also helps the linebackers and tries to stop running plays. The "free safety" lines up behind the middle linebacker and roams as deep or deeper than the deepest receiver. His job is to put the kibosh on big passing or running plays.

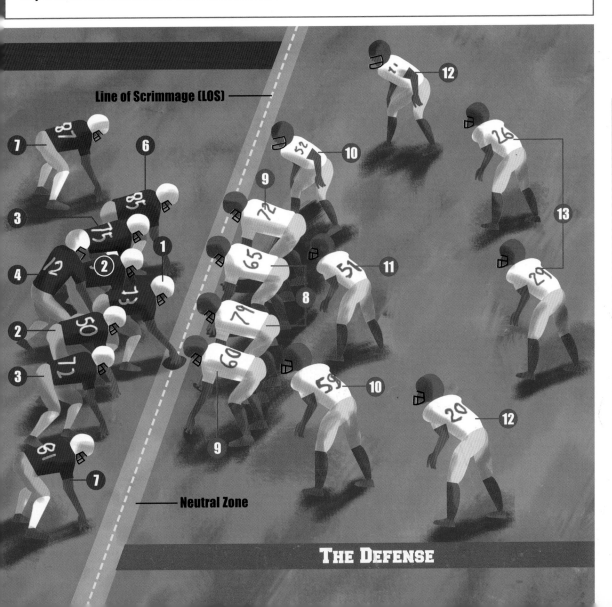

THE DEFENSE

THE QUARTERBACK

When a team wins, the quarterback often gets all the fame and glory. But when it loses, the quarterback often gets all the blame and shame. And those aren't the only things that make the quarterback's job the toughest in pro sports.

> 67, 321, 18 UNDER, 15 PUMP, 145 OVER, LUNCH BOX, 19.5 RHUBARB, 68 DOG BREATH, 3.1415926535897 TO THE POWER OF NINE OVER...

LIGHTS, HUDDLE, ACTION!

In the old days, the quarterback used to call his own plays. But in the 1980s, head coaches took over to relieve quarterbacks of some of the mental pressure of the game. Nowadays, the head coach relays the play over a speaker inside the quarterback's helmet. Then the quarterback calls the play in the huddle just before leading the team to the line of scrimmage. But once they get there, if the quarterback sees that a different play would be better, he may call a play change, or "audible." When he does, he calls the play in a secret code of numbers, letters, and words that only his team knows. For example, the quarterback may yell "5–7–5 pump gut on two." And with that, each player knows exactly what to do. For example, the first three numbers may be routes for specific receivers to run, "pump gut" a pass route for a running back, and "two" the count on which to snap the ball.

ROCKET IN THE POCKET

Hut one! Hut two! Snap goes the football! Once the quarterback receives the snap, the ball is in his hands and it's up to him to make—or break—the play. Talk about pressure! Depending upon what play was called, the quarterback may turn and hand the ball to a running back, run with the ball himself, or drop back into the pocket to pass. The pocket is an area behind the line of scrimmage that the offensive line works hard to protect so the quarterback has time to set up a pass. In the pocket, the quarterback scans the field looking for holes in the defense, throwing lanes to pass the ball through, and receivers that are open for a pass. But he doesn't have long as the opposing team rushes and pushes into the pocket to get him—or at the very least to rattle his cage so that he hurries the pass and blows it. How's that for amping up the pressure?

16

So You Wanna Be a Quarterback...

Do you have what it takes to be a star quarterback? Go through this checklist and see.

√ Able to throw the ball accurately

A quarterback needs a strong arm, a quick release, and bull's-eye accuracy to throw passes to a target receiver faster than the defense can figure out what's hit them.

√ High IQ

Intelligence is a must. An NFL quarterback has to know more than fifty running plays and two hundred passing plays. What's more, the quarterback not only needs to know what he's to do, he also has to know what every other player has to do on each play. That's not all. A quarterback must be able to outwit the defense on the fly.

√ Born to lead

A quarterback must be able to command the troops on the field, inspire teammates by calling competitive plays, and rally players' fighting spirit.

√ Super size

Today, NFL quarterbacks must be big enough to withstand the pounding of punishing hits, and tall enough to see over the heads of huge linemen. According to the experts, that's at least 1.8 m (6 ft. 1 in.) and 95 kg (210 lbs.).

√ Head cool as a cucumber

Boiling over under pressure is a no-no. A quarterback must keep a cool head at all times so he can focus to direct teammates, make plays, find holes in the defense, and retaliate by throwing a long bomb, or pass, into the hands of an open receiver.

√ Nimble and quick

A quarterback must be able to move quickly to set up for a pass, dodge rushing defenders, and run with the ball when required.

Special Forces, er, Teams

Sure, quarterbacks are special. But just who are you going to call if you've got to kick, punt, or return the ball? Special teams for special plays—that's who! A team has several special teams:

- One for kickoffs and punts to pin the opposition close to their own end, and for punt returns to catch the ball, and run with it to gain yards

- One for field goals and extra point attempts (see page 47)

- One for kickoff returns to catch the ball and return it downfield as far as possible

- One for blocking field goals and extra point attempts

STAR ★ • • • • • • • • • • • •

Measuring 1.8 m (5 ft. 10 in.) and weighing just 81.6 kg (180 lbs.), Doug Flutie wasn't the size of a typical pro quarterback. But he held nothing back. In a college game, with his team trailing 45–41 at the 52-yard line with just 6 seconds left on the clock, Flutie threw a long bomb for a touchdown to clinch the game. Is it any wonder *Sports Illustrated* called him "the magic Flutie," or that he went on to quarterback teams in both the NFL and CFL?

Doug Flutie

Quick Hit

If most of the offensive plays that a team makes in a game are runs, they are playing "smashmouth football." But if a team's ace quarterback makes about forty passes, they're playing "air-it-out football."

O nce players set up at the line of scrimmage, the battle is on. The offense tries to move the ball downfield to the end zone to score, and the defense tries to stop them. The offense has four chances (downs) to move the ball 10 yards. If they fail, they give up the ball and the other team goes on offense.

The Offense

Has the advantage.

At the line of scrimmage, the offense knows exactly what they're going to do and the defense doesn't. During the snap count, for example, the offensive players know when the center will hike the ball to the quarterback to start the play, so they can all explode off the line on the count.

Looks for clues.

If the linebackers set themselves up closer to the defensive line, the offense can tell a blitz—when several linebackers or defensive backs join the defensive linemen to rush the quarterback—may be on the way. Spotting a clue like this allows the offense to adjust. For example, the quarterback can quickly pass the ball to a receiver to avoid being tackled with the ball, and the receiver can run a shorter route to catch the ball.

Wants to run the ball.

If the offense can average 4 yards per running play, they'll get 12 yards every three downs—2 more than the 10 yards they need for a new set of downs. Successfully running the ball grinds down the defense, punishes them mentally, and eats time on the clock.

Wants to pass the ball.

Great teams can play both the running game and passing game. That keeps the defense guessing as to what's coming next. And this can open up the game for the offense to make big plays—long passes. Bombs away!

Fakes 'em out.

Sometimes a quarterback steps back as if to pass but instead hands the ball to a running back. This "draw play" may lure the defense to rush the quarterback, which creates holes in the defense for the running back. But sometimes, teams may fake a draw play and the quarterback does fire off a pass. If the ruse makes the defense hesitate, even for a split second, it gives the offense the advantage.

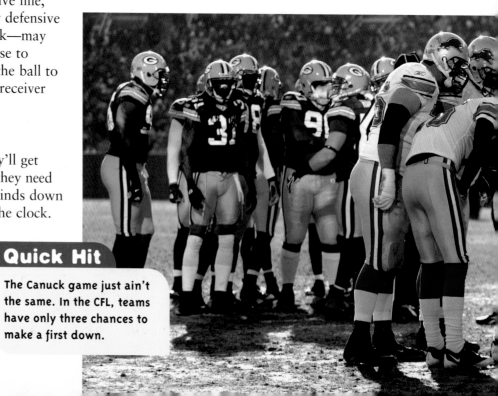

Quick Hit

The Canuck game just ain't the same. In the CFL, teams have only three chances to make a first down.

Has the disadvantage.

The offense knows two things the defense doesn't: the count on which the ball will be snapped and what the play is. The defense can only react, so they surge off the line about a fifth of a second later than the offense. And football games can be won or lost in seconds.

Looks for clues.

Studying the offensive linemen can help the defense figure out whether they are going to run or pass. Say an offensive lineman crouches at the line of scrimmage in a three-point stance, both feet and one hand planted on the ground. If his knuckles and fingertips are white, he's probably about to move forward to block

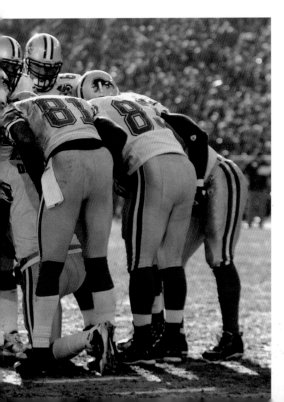

for a run. But on a pass he will move backward to block. The defense also looks in the offensive linemen's eyes: many look in the direction they're about to lunge.

Wants to stop the run.

The defense wants to hold running plays to an average of 3 yards or less, so the offense doesn't gain enough yards for a first down. If the defense stops the run consistently, they also force the offense to pass. Once a pass is airborne, three things can happen: a catch by a receiver, an incompletion, or an interception. And two out of the three ain't bad for the D!

Wants to stop the pass.

And how! The defense rushes the quarterback to sack him, or at least pressure him to make a bad pass. Then there's the bump and run. Even though the rules outlaw hitting receivers as they're running to catch passes, hits on receivers within 5 yards of the line of scrimmage are allowed. So cornerbacks bump receivers as they're coming off the line to disrupt the timing that's critical to catching a pass. Then the cornerbacks turn and run with the receiver.

Fakes 'em out.

Sometimes the defense pulls a stunt at the line of scrimmage. Before the ball is snapped, defensive linemen may jump to one side or switch positions with one another to throw off the offense. Their goal is to confuse the offensive linemen, so they won't know who to block.

Monsters in the Pit

Offensive and defensive linemen do the rough-and-dirty work of football—hitting, ramming, and blocking—in an area at the line of scrimmage called the pit. Check out some of the "monsters" that have ruled the pit.

Purple People Eaters

In the 1960s, the name Vikings wasn't tough enough for the defensive line of the Minnesota Vikings. Maybe that's because the four linemen devoured teams upfront. So people called them the Purple People Eaters, after the Vikings' purple jerseys.

The Hogs

They were large and heavy, and they liked to play mean, in-your-face football in the dirt. So one practice day in the 1980s, when the Washington Redskins' offensive coach said, "Come on you hogs, let's get down here," the name stuck to the offensive linemen like mud.

The Steel Curtain

Ever seen a curtain fall down in the blink of an eye? In the 1970s, the Pittsburgh Steelers' defense earned the nickname the Steel Curtain for bringing down opponents quickly and shutting out touchdowns. In fact, some people say the Steel Curtain is the best defense in NFL history.

William Perry

The Fridge Freezes the Opposition

He was so big that fans called him "The Refrigerator"—or simply "The Fridge." At his heaviest, 1.9 m (6 ft. 2 in.) defensive tackle William Perry rocked the scales at a whopping 173 kg (382 lbs.). What's more, Perry played for the Chicago Bears in the 1980s, when linemen who topped 136 kg (300 lbs.) were a rare item.

Perry's massive heft made him unstoppable. The defensive tackle plowed through opponents' offense and even did double duty as a fullback, carrying the ball or blocking, clearing the way for a running back with the ball. During Super Bowl XX, the Bears were on a third down at the 1-yard line in the third quarter when coach Mike Ditka sent in The Fridge to freeze the opposition.

The Fridge took a handoff from quarterback Jim McMahon and rammed through a stunned defensive line into the end zone for a touchdown. *Wahoo!* Chicago won the game and Perry got to chill out with a Super Bowl ring fit for a king, er, fridge. The Refrigerator's ring was a record-setting size 25—more than twice the ring size of the average guy. Now that's big bling!

Chapter 3

THE FIELD

Perfect, "turf-ect"! Not a mark or a bald spot to break up the "field of green." Not a lump or a bump to throw players off course. Not a hole or a mole to trip players up. Not a divot or a piece missing in action. Nothing less will do for the turf of pro football.

And here's the rub. When a football field is perfect, no one seems to notice. But when it is not up to snuff, it may make the national news as the coaches, the players, and even the fans complain.

Sounding off about the condition of the field is a good ol' football tradition. After all, the game is played mainly in open-air stadiums, whatever the weather. Check out how the turf has rolled out through time, how groundskeepers maintain the field, and how some teams have turned the turf into a home field advantage.

"Turf's Up!" ➤

HOW TURF FLIES

T ufts of turf sure do fly as players run and dig their cleats into fields of natural grass. But that's not all. Turf also flies like time as trends take off around the league and natural grass and artificial turfs go in and out of style. Here's how the different surfaces have rolled out through time.

1860s

Real grass is the battleground for the world's first football matches and the game is played on nothing but for the next 100 years.

1965

The first domed stadium, the Houston Astrodome, rises up. People call it the eighth wonder of the world. The only problem is the grass doesn't get enough sunlight to grow and it croaks.

1966

Got a field of dead grass and painted-green dirt? Roll out the green carpet! Fake grass made of plastic, which becomes known as Astroturf, replaces the natural grass at the Astrodome.

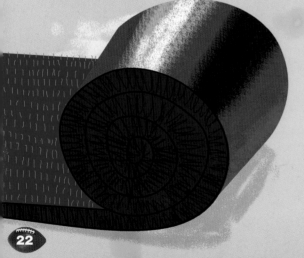

1968

The Astrodome becomes the home turf of the Houston Oilers and with that, Astroturf becomes all the rage in pro football. The big leagues like it because it looks great on TV. Owners like it because it doesn't need to be cut, watered, and fertilized like grass. Coaches and players like it because it's free of hazardous holes and divots players could twist their ankles in.

1970s

Astroturf becomes a sore spot for players. No kidding! As players run, jump, cut, tackle, and fall, they take a real beating. That's because Astroturf is a thin plastic covering on top of asphalt—a much harder surface than grass, with less give. What's more, when players slide on Astroturf, they get a "rug burn" on their skin. And to top it all off, sometimes players' feet can get caught in a seam between two pieces of the green "carpet."

1980s

Studies begin to show that playing on artificial turf is more likely to cause serious injuries than playing on real grass.

1990

More than half the NFL stadiums have artificial turf, and it's changed the game. Coaches and players say that the ball rolls faster and players run faster on artificial turf. The newfound speed allows quarterbacks, running backs, and wide receivers to take control of the game. The result? The search for speedy players becomes teams' number one priority.

1995

Natural grass starts to re-sprout on fields around the league as yet more studies show that playing on artificial turf is more likely to result in injuries.

2001

In the winter, as much as 1 m (2 ½ ft.) of snow often piles up on the Denver Broncos' playing field, which is 1.6 km (1 mi.) above sea level. To help the grass survive, the Broncos inject twenty million artificial grass fibers into their field. As the grass grows, it entwines with the artificial fibers and this strengthens and anchors the turf.

2002

The Seattle Seahawks install FieldTurf, a new artificial turf that looks and feels like real grass, at their new stadium. The turf gets rave reviews and NFL teams start ripping up their old artificial turf to "resod" with the new stuff.

Around 2009

A survey of NFL players reveals that almost three-quarters prefer playing on natural grass than artificial turf. In another survey, the players' most common comment is "make all fields grass to prevent injuries."

2010

In the NFL, natural grass playing fields outnumber artificial turf playing fields about two to one.

WHAT TURF WILL FLY NEXT?

Green blades and ham? No one knows for sure. But experts say new turf developments are happening all the time.

Quick Answers to Hard-Hitting Questions

What makes new artificial turf feel like real grass?

The new turf's blades of "grass" are made of softer fibers than those of Astroturf and they don't cause rug burn as players slide on them. The new turf also has a built-in cushion of sand and rubber granules made out of recycled tires. This cushion has more "give" than Astroturf, compressing to soften on impact as players' feet and bodies hit the turf.

Is the world, er, field flat?

Nope. A good football field is gently sloped in the center to encourage rainwater to run off and drain away.

H ow many college or pro players play the whole game?" Tennessee Titans' groundskeeper Terry Porch once asked. "None, right? But this field has to play every down… So you can imagine what happens out there in the middle with 300-pound guys in cleats." Once the game is over, the beat-up blades need some TLC from the ground crew to recover. Check out how teams keep natural grass in tip-top playing condition.

MEET MURPH THE TURF

I t may sound crazy, but some teams treat the turf just like a person to keep the grass healthy.

The crew gives the turf regular "haircuts." They spend hours mowing the grass several times a week. This keeps the grass short and "burns in" the pattern of light and dark stripes you see on the field.

The ground crew feeds and waters the grass regularly. In fact, grass can "eat" as much as 350 kg (775 lbs.) of fertilizer a year.

After a game, the ground crew is ready with seed and new sod to clean up the grass and tend to its cuts and bruises—a.k.a. divots and cleat marks—which number in the hundreds. And if the grass turns brown or gets sick, they may call in the turf doc (see right).

PAINT BY NUMBER?

W ell, not exactly. But the ground crew does use stencils and string to paint the numbers, hash marks, and yard lines on the field. The crew pulls a taut string down the length of the field to create a straight line. Then they place stencils of the numbers and hash marks along the string and spray white paint over the stencils. They go up and down both sides of the field. A hash mark is spray painted at every yard, a solid white line at every 5th yard, and a number at every 10th yard line. The crosshatch of white lines that they create is what gives the field its nickname: the gridiron. Since mowing the field cuts off the painted tips of the grass, crews may paint the field a few times a week!

Lines didn't appear on the football field until 1882, when a new rule required teams to gain 5 yards on three downs to keep possession of the ball. They used chalk to draw a line at every 5th yard.

TURNING UP THE HEAT

How do you coax lush, green grass to grow in December? Turn up the heat! No joke. As the NFL season heads into winter, ground crews face the challenge of keeping the grass looking good in the stadium and on TV—not to mention soft and stable beneath players' feet. So some ground crews, like those of the Chicago Bears and the Green Bay Packers, fire up turf-conditioning systems installed in the ground underneath the field. The systems heat the roots of the grass by pumping hot water through the thousands of feet of underground plastic tubing. This warms the root zone of the grass and can even melt snow on the field when the air temperature hovers around the freezing mark. That way fans can still see the gridiron to follow the action and, more importantly, the field remains safe and relatively soft for the players during freezing conditions.

Turf Doc to the Rescue

Grass is a living thing, and if it doesn't get what it needs, football teams can't count on it to "play by the rules." Nobody knows that better than George Toma (below), an NFL groundskeeper who has earned a place in the Football Hall of Fame for excellent field maintenance, and has tended the field for the Super Bowl since 1965. In fact, when grass dies or doesn't take root, NFL teams often call in Toma to the rescue. Take the San Francisco 49ers, who found themselves playing on grass that had no roots. In the 1990s, after two weeks of record rainfall that triggered mud slides in California, the 49ers' field was a mess of sodden mud. Toma got to work on the field, growing a test plot of a grass called kukuya. The grass stood up well in a game played in the pouring rain. So he had the *kukuya* grass cut from another field nearby and sodded the 49ers' field with it. And the field held up beautifully in the next few games played in the rain. The fans even gave the ground crew a standing ovation.

"TURF OPS"

Ever heard the term "special ops" for special operations forces that carry out important military missions in the field? Sometimes football teams deploy special operations to try to gain a home field advantage. Check out some sneaky moves of "turf ops" in action.

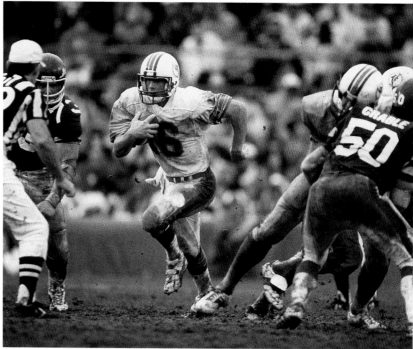

PATRIOTS PULL A SNOW JOB

On December 12, 1982, a heavy snowstorm raged over the New England Patriots' turf as the squad squared off against the Miami Dolphins. A blanket of snow covered the field so completely that none of the players could see the markings, yard lines, or sidelines. Both teams missed field goals as 23 cm (9 in.) of snow piled up on the field. With about five minutes left to go and the score 0–0, the Patriots found themselves within reach of a field goal and called a timeout. Suddenly, a makeshift snowplow—a tractor with a broom tacked onto the front—slid onto the field, clearing a 1.2 m (4 ft.) wide patch for Patriots' kicker John Smith. Dolphins' coach Don Shula protested fiercely. But to no avail. *Boom!* The kick was good and the Patriots won the game. The next spring though, the NFL outlawed the snowplow shenanigans with a rule that says groundskeepers cannot clear snow before a kick.

MUD BOWL IN MIAMI

According to NFL lore, it wasn't long before the Miami Dolphins' coach Don Shula ordered a sneaky "turf op" of his own. During the 1982–83 playoffs, the Dolphins were set to meet the New York Jets. Shula knew that the Jets' superior speed gave them an edge over the Dolphins. To slow the Jets down and take away their edge in speed, Shula told the ground crew to leave the field uncovered throughout a solid week of rain before the game in Miami. On game day, both teams struggled to play in the resultant "bowl of mud" and remained scoreless in the first half. Then Miami managed to light up the scoreboard and even shut out the Jets, earning a spot in the Super Bowl. Who knew the weather before a game—the rain on the plain—could be used as a secret weapon?

GRASS NOT GREENER IN PITTSBURGH

In 2007, NFL players rated Heinz Field, the home of the Pittsburgh Steelers, as the worst grass field in the league. When Heinz Field opened in 2001, the Steelers laid down natural grass. After that, they resurfaced the field several times, even adding artificial fibers to help hold the grass in place. But maybe having a reputation for the worst grass field in the league is exactly the way Pitttsburgh's club President Art Rooney likes it. "If people come in thinking these aren't ideal conditions and that's always in the back of their minds, who knows how it affects their performance?" Rooney once asked. "We tell our kickers, 'Make sure you tell the opposing kickers this is the worst field you've ever kicked off.'" How's that for playing mind games on the field?

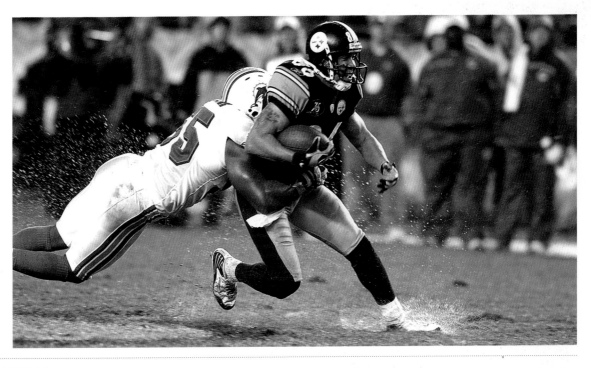

BENCHES HEAT UP THE GAME

When the Cleveland Browns were set to meet the Oakland Raiders in the 1980 playoffs, the Browns thought they had home field advantage in more ways than one. That's because they didn't have heated benches on the sidelines, where frigid winter temperatures often froze opposing players, who just weren't used to the big chill. But Oakland Raiders' owner Al Davis was wise to that and borrowed heated benches for the match. And the benches turned up the heat on the game. In fact, the NFL ruled that Davis had to bring in heated benches for Cleveland as well. But it turned out to be worth the extra effort for Davis. The Raiders won the game 14–12.

STAR ★ • • • • • • • • • • • • • • • • • • •

Tom Brady has led the New England Patriots to not one but three Super Bowl victories. In 2002, during his first playoff game, even driving snow could not hold the star quarterback back. As the Patriots faced the Oakland Raiders, snow covered the field and made the ball slick to handle. Nevertheless, Brady completed a thrilling 32 passes for 312 yards and even ran the ball into the Raiders' end zone for a touchdown, spearheading the Patriots to a 16–13 win. You might say Brady threw snow in the face of the Raiders.

Tom Brady

27

LEGENDS OF THE GAME

Bart Starr

The Ice Bowl Rocks the Game

Slip, sliding, and shivering away! That's what the Green Bay Packers and the Dallas Cowboys were doing at the NFL Championship game in 1967. Not only did a solid sheet of ice cover the field, but high winds blasted it, and the wind chill made it feel like 40 below. The whistle even froze to the referee's lips!

During the off-season, the Packers had installed an electric heating grid under their field to keep the grass warm and dry during cold and snowy winter weather. So when Packers' groundskeepers heard frigid temperatures forecast for the big game, they turned on the electric grid and put a tarp over the field for extra protection. And that's what caused the most brutal field conditions pro football has ever seen.

Overnight, heat from the grid formed water droplets, or condensation, on the tarp. So when groundskeepers lifted off the tarp on game day, the droplets ran onto the grass and froze, instantly turning the field into a virtual skating rink. Players struggled to get a firm footing on the field. And though Green Bay grabbed an early scoring lead,

the Cowboys came storming back and slid ahead 17–14. With less than five minutes left in the fourth quarter, Green Bay quarterback Bart Starr led a scoring drive that moved the Packers all the way from their 32-yard line to the Cowboy's 1-foot yardline. After a few fumbles and slips, Starr managed to fake a handoff to a running back, hang onto the ball, and dive headfirst into the end zone. Touchdown on ice!

Is it any wonder the Super Bowl is rarely played in places with cool winter climates anymore?

Chapter 4

THE COMPLETE ATHLETE

Grunt! Squat! Lift those dumbbells! You can do it. Now, hit the deck for forty pushups. Lunge, turn, lunge. Do ten high-knees, driving your knees into your chest, ten buttkicks, ten jumping jacks, and the list goes on and on.... The daily workouts of pro players are action-packed all right, as some perform seventy or more moves and exercises. Is it any wonder that some modern football pros can bench-press, or lift, 250 kg (550 lbs.) and run 40 yards in just 4.2 seconds flat?

Long gone is the era when pro football players could play baseball in the off-season and use training camp to shape up for the season. Nowadays, pro football players grind it out in the gym all year round. Get the scoop on how the pros train their bodies and minds to meet the punishing demands of the battle on the gridiron.

Get Fit!

Getting into first-rate playing shape is a big job. Since 1985, the average NFL player's weight has ballooned ten percent to a whopping 112 kg (248 lbs). But this super-size doesn't mean a thing unless they have the strength, speed, and endurance to back it up.

SHAPING UP FOR FOOTBALL

Hit and run. That's what football players do most on the gridiron. In fact, some players describe the game as a series of traffic accidents. After all, opposing players set up on the line of scrimmage and run and smash into each other on each and every play. *Slam, bam, wham!* And their bodies often pile up on top of each other in a big heap on the field. Oh sure, players also throw, catch, and kick the ball, and they need to practice these skills to perfect them. But physical conditioning for football focuses on building strength and speed. Players need the strength to hit and take hits from opponents, no matter what their size. They also need the speed to boot it down the 100-yard field in seconds flat carrying the ball or to catch an opponent with the ball and take him down.

TRAIN TO GAIN

Whether you're playing for your school team or in the big leagues, the secret of success for all athletes is the same: train, train, train. To build the strength and speed they need, pro players work out with the team each week during the season, pumping iron and running sprints. Many also work with a personal trainer, especially in the off-season. Their personal trainers design workouts to challenge individual weaknesses and build on strengths. And some players will do whatever it takes to gain an edge on opponents. For example, part of defensive end Dwight Freeney's fitness routine is to do pushups with 40 kg (90 lbs.) of thick chains on top of his back. Freeney also pulls a giant tire along the ground like a bull pulls a plow. No joke! Other players are cagey about their workouts. For example, when rocket-footed running back LaDainian Tomlinson, a.k.a. L.T., was interviewed by the TV show *60 Minutes*, he wouldn't let them see part of his routine designed by his personal trainer. How's that for a top-secret trade secret? He also works with a massage therapist and doctor to help repair muscle damage from injuries. Talk about total body conditioning!

THE FUEL

Everybody knows you can't run and jump without any fuel in your tank. But that doesn't mean eating everything in sight to "bulk up." Lugging around extra weight will slow you down and make you less agile. To make sure NFL players get the proper nutrients and energy they need, teams have a cafeteria where they eat together during the practice week and chow down a pre-game meal on game day.

NFL teams serve up rice or pasta with every meal, so players can load up on complex carbohydrates. Team meals also include a mound of vegetables, fruit, and a small piece of meat on the side.

The team eats the pre-game meal about three to four hours before the game, so they have ample time to digest it. But it's the meal that players eat the night before the game that gives them the fuel to go all out during the game—as long as it's balanced in the following "pro-portions:"

60% carbohydrates. Rice, pasta, cereals, breads, vegetables, and fruit are players' main source of energy. Carbohydrates provide fuel for intense exercise and help keep players going during a game's last thirty minutes, when many wins and losses are decided.

20% proteins. Proteins from lean meats and fish, as well as peanut butter, eggs, grains, nuts, and seeds, help players build and repair their muscles.

20% "good" fats. Fats from red meat, cheese, eggs, milk, butter, salad dressing, nuts, and seeds get stored in the body as potential energy. Once carbohydrate energy gets low, fats begin to supply energy. They also help muscles develop and provide a protective cushion for players' inner organs.

WHAT'S UP DOC?

Smack! Two players collide full on. **Bam!** A player tackles an opponent and slams him on the ground. **Whack!** A player's head smashes into an opponent's knee. **Ouch!** Football is a collision sport all right, and injuries are part of the game.

PLAYING THROUGH PAIN

Before Super Bowl XLIV, all eyes were on Dwight Freeney (below). Would the Indianapolis Colts' big defensive end, known for explosive speed, recover from a sprained ankle in time to play? The scuttlebutt was that Freeney had a third-degree sprain with a torn ligament, or connective tissue. But nobody was more determined than Freeney. He put in seventeen hours of rehab a day. He iced the swollen ankle over and over. He lay in a hyperbaric chamber, a sealed tube that combines high air pressure with pure oxygen to pump lots of oxygen to the injury to help it heal faster. He also used a device to pump extra blood to the injury. And when the big game started, Freeney took the field and gave everything he had. He busted out into his signature speedy spin and even dropped opposing quarterback Drew Brees into the dirt. However, by halftime, Freeney's ankle stiffened up and didn't come back to life enough for Freeney to be his usual force to reckon with. Nevertheless, Freeney gave his all for all four quarters of the game.

CONKED IN THE HEAD!

What do quarterback Kurt Warner and running back Clinton Portis have in common besides playing pro football? They've both been knocked out of the lineup by a concussion—a chemical imbalance in the brain caused by a blow to the head. The human brain sits inside the skull like a person sitting in a car without a seatbelt. If your head gets hit, your skull stops or twists suddenly. Since the brain has nothing holding it in place, it crashes inside of the skull. *Wham!* This sets off a chain of chemical reactions that can cause dizziness, memory loss, headaches, balance problems—even personality changes or brain damage. Symptoms can be very subtle, which makes concussions hard to diagnose. However, recent research shows that suffering several concussions can lead to brain damage, so now the NFL encourages players to come forward with head injuries. And a neurologist—a doctor who specializes in the nervous system, which contains the brain—must test the players to make sure they are free of symptoms before they can return to the action.

Playing football can be really draining! Offensive linemen and defensive backs can lose as much as 7 kg (15 lbs.) of water weight during a single game.

Quick Answers to Hard-Hitting Questions

What's the injury report?

To prevent "inside information" from giving gamblers betting on the game or teams an edge, NFL teams must file weekly reports on injured players. The report lists injured players, the injured body parts, whether players took part in practice, and if they are likely to play in the next game. But filling out the report is a game itself. For example, to disclose as little meaningful information as possible to opponents, some teams list almost every player as having an injury. Others list almost none. And some will even list the wrong injuries on purpose.

Are pro players pumped up on steroids?

Steroids are drugs that can help people build larger muscles than we can build naturally. In an anonymous survey in 2009, about one in ten retired NFL players admitted they had used steroids while playing. Today, NFL rules ban the use of steroids. Not only can steroids give players an unfair advantage over competitors, but studies show the drugs can lead to more injuries as players' bodies don't adapt fast enough or well enough to the bigger muscles they develop. These drugs have many other side effects, which can lead to serious long-term health problems. So it doesn't pay to use drugs to play.

DRIP, DRIP, AND LET IT RIP

It's not easy keeping cool on the gridiron, especially in the southern states where temperatures of 54°C (130°F) or more may practically bake the field. After all, football players lug around 9 kg (20 lbs.) of equipment with every step they take. And their equipment and uniforms cover all their skin except for their face, neck, and part of their forearms. What's more, their helmets put their body's natural cooling system on the fritz by trapping heat that normally escapes through the head. Players can overheat and lose body fluids easily through sweating, so trainers constantly remind them to drink water and sports drinks on the sidelines and even to increase the amount they drink the week before the game. Nevertheless, some players get heat stroke or severe bouts of dehydration in which all their muscles cramp up. During halftime or after the game, the team doctor hooks up these players to an intravenous (IV) drip bag to quickly replace lost fluids, sugar, salt, potassium, and electrolytes. *Drip, drip, drip....*

THE MIND

Some players rehearse plays through the technique of *visualization*. They watch mental movies of themselves successfully making a play over and over, so these pictures take root in their minds and they can make the play instinctively in games. Does it work? Studies show that athletes who do visualization and physical practice outperform those who do not. Check out how else players train their minds.

IMAGINE THIS...

You are a defensive back covering a shifty wide receiver who has a knack for making seemingly impossible catches. The opposing quarterback throws a long pass, and the ball hangs in the air above both of your heads for what seems like forever. Can you knock the ball away before the receiver gets his hands on it? Or maybe even intercept it? But what if you blow it? What if you don't jump in time...?

MONKEY THINK, MONKEY DO

Gotcha! Before you know it, the receiver has leapt up and made the catch, and you and your feet are on the ground. Your thoughts distracted you and you blew it. "I'm such a loser," you say to yourself. Stop right there. Don't get down on yourself. According to sports psychologists, your thoughts rule your actions. If you think you won't jump in time, for example, your body will follow. What's more, research studies show that athletes' thoughts and self-talk—things they say to themselves as they perform—influence their success. Researchers believe that negative thoughts can lead to poor play, while positive thoughts can give players the chance to play well. So instead of focusing on what went wrong, focus on what went right—like the fact that you stuck with the receiver all the way downfield and now you've got a chance to tackle him and shake the ball loose.

FOOTBALL IS SO MENTAL

Experts say that talent and physical skills are pretty much even among top football players and that what separates the best from the rest is mental toughness. The fact is, when players begin to lose confidence in their abilities through negative thoughts or self-talk, their muscles tense up and they can no longer perform to the best of their abilities. So pro players train their minds to develop mental toughness and use positive thoughts to remain focused even in pressure-filled situations. First, players identify the negative thoughts and self-talk that run through their minds during games. Then players replace these with positive thoughts and statements and practice saying the statements over and over. Players may also write them out, post them in their locker, tape them on their mirror, and even record them on their MP3 player to listen to them over and over. That way, when players make a mistake in a game, they don't fall apart. The positive thoughts and self-talk refocus them, so they can keep their heads in the game. Talk about being mental!

Quick Hit

Does the way you think stink? Players and team psychologists often call negative thoughts that go through players' minds in game situations "stinking thinking."

Gotta Have Heart

Sure, you need size, strength, speed, tip-top physical conditioning, and a good mental attitude to excel on the gridiron. But don't underestimate the power of heart. Experts say that desire is a key ingredient of athletic success. A strong desire to play can motivate athletes with less talent to outperform those with exceptional talent. Take running back DeAngelo Williams. People have always told him that he's not big enough for football, and going into the NFL 2006 draft it was no different. "A lot of teams looked at me and thought 'He's a third-string back at best,'" Williams once said. But in 2008, Williams cracked the starting lineup for the Carolina Panthers and set the field ablaze. The determined running back rushed for 1515 yards and eighteen touchdowns on 273 carries. "It's just a testament that they can measure your height, they can measure your weight, and they can somewhat measure your skill," said Williams. "But they can never measure the size of a man's heart."

TRY THIS!

How can you remain cool, calm, and collected on the outside when you have butterflies in your stomach on the inside? Try this experiment and see.

YOU WILL NEED
• a high-pressure situation where you feel nervous

1 When you feel under pressure, take a deep breath.

2 Act as if you feel perfectly fine and smile.

3 Notice how smiling makes you feel inside.

Why does smiling help you "fake it until you make it"?

Answer on page 64.

Quick Answers to Hard-Hitting Questions

What does it mean for players to "give 110 percent"?

Experts say that there is only one way to play football: to go all out. Not only must players play with their minds and bodies, they must play with their hearts. Emotional energy, will, and desire can drive a player to achieve incredible physical feats, like rushing through a maze of opponents for a touchdown with an opponent clinging to his back.

STAR ★ • • • • • • • • • • •

Who's the greatest receiver of all time? Chances are any coach, TV announcer, or journalist will say Jerry Rice. From 1985 to 2004, the star wide receiver set NFL records for the most receptions, receiving yards, touchdown receptions, and touchdowns. What set Rice apart from other players was his desire. He never let up. He kept coming at the defense with the same level of intensity throughout the entire game. This wore down defenders and they wavered, opening up the field an inch or two for Rice to make big plays.

Jerry Rice

LEGENDS OF THE GAME

Drew Brees

Brees and the Saints Go Marching In

When Drew Brees signed with the New Orleans Saints in 2006, the city was still reeling from Hurricane Katrina. More than three-quarters of New Orleans lay in ruins underwater in the wake of one of the deadliest hurricanes to ever hit the U.S. And maybe Brees fit right in. The quarterback was recovering from a devastating shoulder injury. In fact, some people thought he would never play again.

But people had always underestimated Brees. In high school, he didn't lose a single football game he played. Nevertheless, a college scholarship was hard to come by. In college, Brees led his team to their first Rose Bowl in thirty-four years, setting a record for career passing yards along the way. Yet doubts about his abilities still dogged him. People said he was too short for a quarterback—a mere 1.8 m (6 ft.). They said he didn't have a strong arm, and "yadda, yadda, yadda."

What they failed to see was that Brees is an amazing athlete who is quick on his feet and mentally tough, with great hand-eye coordination. When the TV show *Sports Science* measured Brees's accuracy in throwing footballs at a target, Brees was more accurate than top archers. He hit the bull's-eye ten out of ten times.

What's more, Brees has a work ethic and motivation like no other. Brees put in four solid months of grueling seven-hour days of rehab to recover against all odds and play again. As he rebuilt himself as a player, he helped rebuild New Orleans and give the city something to cheer about. Within four years, he led the Saints to their first Super Bowl victory. Is it any wonder people started to call him "the miracle man"?

Chapter 5

PREPARING FOR BATTLE

Snap, buckle, pop! Smear on the grease, er, glop! Football players gear up from head to toe much like ancient gladiators once clad themselves in armor to step into the ring with lions. But it wasn't always so.

In the early days of football, players went head to head without helmets or pads of any kind. No joke! In the 1870s, the standard football uniform was a canvas smock worn over a team jersey, pants made of padded canvas or thick cotton, wool stockings, and high-top shoes with leather spikes. However, it wasn't long before players began stuffing leather shin guards down their stockings for protection from kicks and blows. Discover how helmets evolved to protect players' heads, how modern players gear up to take to the battlefield, and how NFL teams bone up on their enemies—a.k.a. their opponent of the week.

Michael Robinson,
San Francisco 49ers

Let the Battle Begin!

MODERN GLADIATORS GEAR UP

 When you gear up for a battle on the gridiron, you'd better cover your body from head to toe. Check out the "armor" players wear to protect nearly every body part.

A Real Head Case

You don't have to be a head case to play football, but pros don't leave the locker room without one. Huh? It is an NFL rule to wear a helmet on the field at all times. Helmets have a hard plastic shell, and they are fitted to an individual player's head to provide maximum protection from the kicks and blows of the game.

A Skintight Jersey

Players' jerseys are made of nylon, with spandex on the sides for a skintight fit. So there's not much for an opponent to grab onto. In fact, some jerseys worn by offensive and defensive linemen are so tight that the players need help to get them on and off. Some linemen even spray their jerseys with non-stick cooking spray to help them slip through opponents' fingers.

Pants that Rule

Football pants are made of nylon and spandex. They are designed to hug players' lower bodies and to hold the hip, thigh, and knee pads underneath the pants. According to NFL rules, the jersey must be tucked into the pants at all times. So players' pants have a wide strip of Velcro inside the waistband that sticks to Velcro at the back of the jersey. The pants also house an extension of the bottom of the jersey that wraps from front to back for extra "tucked-in" insurance. That's not all the "ants" in football pants. Some players have even worn nylons under their pants for warmth on cold days.

Smudges 'n' Stickers

As players gear up for battle, many apply a smudge of grease or a sticker beneath each eye. Is it all just for show? Recent studies show that the grease does improve visibility by absorbing light and cutting down glare. But the stickers don't. Nevertheless, no one knows whether eye black actually gives players a leg up, er, eye up in games.

Socks to Rock

Players wear one-piece socks or stockings. According to NFL rules, socks must cover the entire leg from the bottom of the pants to the shoe. What's more, the sock must be white from the top of the shoe to the middle of the calf. How's that for a strict sock code?

A Shoulder to Hit On

Underneath their jerseys, players wear shoulder pads made of a hard plastic shell and foam padding. The pads protect the shoulders, chest, and ribs. Some players, like quarterbacks, running backs, and wide receivers add a flak jacket that looks like a vest for extra rib protection. Other players, like linemen, add attachments that make their pads difficult for opponents to use as handholds. Players can add foam padding for extra protection. The pads absorb the shock of hits by deforming on impact. They also spread out the shock over a larger area, which reduces the pressure at the point of impact.

If the Glove Fits...

Different players with different jobs choose different gloves. Linemen wear gloves thick with padding to protect their hands and fingers, which can get stuck in other players' face masks or stepped on by a pile of feet. Receivers wear tact gloves with a sticky rubber palm, or gloves covered with a sticky substance like rosin or a spray, to help them catch the ball. Nevertheless, NFL rules forbid players from applying any type of sticky gel or "stick 'em" to their gloves or their bodies. Go figure!

Shoes for All Fields

On natural grass, pros wear shoes with cleats, or plastic screw-in spikes, that allow them to dig into the field. And the wetter the grass, the longer the cleats they wear. In fact, equipment managers use electric screwdrivers to change players' cleats to match changing field conditions during games. On artificial turf, players wear shoes with rubber cleats to match the field conditions, or shoes without cleats. Who knew football could be so choosy about its "shoesies"?

Suiting up in Armor

Hip pads, thigh pads, knee pads, elbow pads, and a tailbone pad are all part of a football player's armor, along with a jockstrap. The pads come in a variety of styles, depending on players' position, personal preferences, and injuries.

STAR ★ · · · · · · · · · · · · ·

No cornerback stuck his hands on the ball quite like Lester Hayes did in 1980. The star defender picked off thirteen passes in the regular season and five more in the playoffs, two of which he ran in for touchdowns. What's more, Hayes shut down opponents' receivers by sticking to them like glue. No kidding! Hayes slathered a gooey yellowish brown substance called Stickum all over his jersey, arms, wrists, and hands. Maybe the NFL thought too many players and passes just got stuck on Hayes, because the league banned Stickum in 1981.

Lester Hayes

Tape It and Take It, Dude!

Did you know it's a league rule for players to have their ankles taped before playing a game? Taping their ankles gives players extra support and protection. So players tape their ankles for practices and many tape other body parts as well. In fact, the average NFL team uses up more than 480 km (300 mi.) of tape in a single season. And get this: in the 1960s and 1970s, some defensive linemen taped hockey pucks and ashtrays to their hands to sock it to their opponents on the field of battle.

THE HELMET

 o piece of protective football equipment is as important as the helmet. Without one, a hit to the head can result in a concussion that knocks players out of the game, and may even scramble their brains.

A HELMET THAT FITS JUST RIGHT

A football helmet is not your average lid, dude. It has several parts—a hard plastic shell, jaw pads, inflatable air bladders, a face mask, a chin strap, and a mouth guard—that come in different styles and sizes so players can mix and match to fit their noodle best. An equipment manager helps each player choose a shell by measuring the player's head with a pair of calipers. Then they add foam pads and inflatable air pads inside the top and sides to make sure the helmet fits snugly. The player puts on the helmet and the equipment manager pumps up the air pads through holes in the shell.

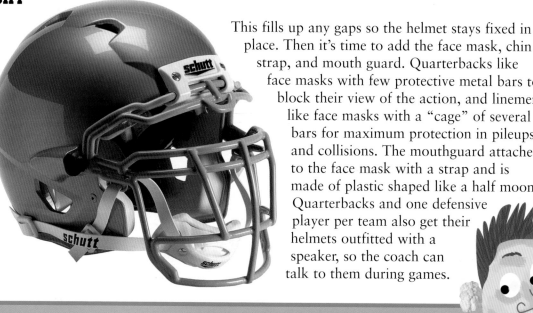

This fills up any gaps so the helmet stays fixed in place. Then it's time to add the face mask, chin strap, and mouth guard. Quarterbacks like face masks with few protective metal bars to block their view of the action, and linemen like face masks with a "cage" of several bars for maximum protection in pileups and collisions. The mouthguard attaches to the face mask with a strap and is made of plastic shaped like a half moon. Quarterbacks and one defensive player per team also get their helmets outfitted with a speaker, so the coach can talk to them during games.

HEADS 'N' HELMETS ROLL THROUGH TIME

Check out how helmets have evolved to protect players' heads through time.

1890s
Ads appear for football skullcaps made of silk to protect players' hair and ears.

1891
Players' ears are easy targets for boxing and pulling by opponents. James Naismith, the inventor of basketball, designs ear muffs to protect players' ears, when he plays center for his school's football team in Springfield, Massachusetts.

1893
A doctor tells football player Admiral Joseph Mason Reeves that another kick to the head might kill him or turn him into a vegetable. So Reeves has a shoemaker make a leather helmet and wears it to play.

1896
Halfback George Barclay lives in fear of getting a "cauliflower ear" from a blow to the head. So a harness maker makes him a leather hat that covers his ears. And so Barclay wears the first head harness into the game. And early helmets that trickle onto the field become known as head harnesses.

Gear to Cheer

Check out some of the whackiest head gear around that not one but thousands of fans wear in the stands.

The Cheeseheads Are Here

The fans of the Green Bay Packers don head gear like no other—foam hats that look like giant wedges of Swiss cheese. Before the hats existed, people called the Packers' fans "cheeseheads" as an insult because the team's home state, Wisconsin, produces more than 9 million tonnes (2 billion lbs.) of cheese a year. In the late 1980s, a man made a cheese hat out of an old couch cushion, and soon cheesehead hats began bobbing up and down in the Green Bay stands. And so the Packers' fans turned the cheesy insult on its head!

Invasion of the Melon Snatchers

When fans of the Saskatchewan Rough Riders arrived in Calgary for the 2009 Grey Cup championship game, there was a run on watermelons in grocery stores throughout the city. Some stores even ordered in special shipments so fans could gear up for the game. What was up with that? Rough Riders' fans like to scoop out a watermelon, cut the rind into a helmet, and stick it on their heads to wear at the game. How's that for cool headgear?

STAR ★

Emmitt Smith had an uncanny nose for holes in his opponent's defense. In 1995, the star running back slipped past defenders for a record-setting twenty-five rushing touchdowns in one season. Once over the goal line, Smith would rip off his helmet to celebrate. And though the NFL quashed his helmet dance in 1997 with the "Emmitt Smith rule," which calls for a 15-yard penalty if a player removes his helmet on the field, nobody could stop Smith from scoring.

Emmitt Smith

Around 1917

Helmets: some players wear one and some players don't. But helmets offer better protection as a suspension system to absorb shocks is added.

1920s

Hinkey Haines dons a leather helmet for full face protection.

1940s

Helmet makers begin making football helmets out of plastic and add the first face masks.

1970s

Pump it up! The first inflatable liners appear in football helmets.

Beyond

Will helmets with a sensor, or thermistor, to measure players' skin temperature become required gear?

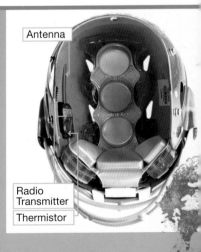

Antenna

Radio Transmitter

Thermistor

THE WEEKLY GRIND

S hort and oh-so-sweet. That's what the football season is. Unlike the grueling eighty-two-game schedule of pro hockey and basketball, NFL players play only sixteen times. And often only once a week, usually on Sunday. But that doesn't make football any less of a grind. Players spend an entire week planning and practicing to beat their opponents. Check out a week in the life of a pro team.

Quick Hit

The scribbles and diagrams of x's and o's found in a team's playbook look like ancient Egyptian hieroglyphics to the average Joe or Jane. Nevertheless, by the end of the season, other teams have most of it figured out from watching films of the team play.

VICTORY MONDAY?

If the team won last Sunday's game, the coach may give them the day off—a.k.a. Victory Monday. But if not, the players have to show up for work.

8:00 a.m. All players must attend a team breakfast.

8:30 a.m. The coaching staff meet to begin writing the playbook for their next opponent (see Players Hit the Books, right).

9:00 a.m. Victory Monday or not, any injured players report to the team doc for examination, re-evaluation, and treatment of yesterday's injuries.

9:30 a.m. Healthy players work out: stretch sore muscles, run cross-country, and lift weights.

11:00 a.m. Lunchtime! Players refuel in the team cafeteria.

11:30 a.m. Meetings begin. Teams may have a Special Teams meeting so the entire team sees what each player contributes to the team in his role as a punter, kick returner, or the like.

12:00 p.m. The head coach guides the team through all the things in yesterday's game that helped them win or lose.

12:30 p.m. The team breaks up into offensive and defensive teams and each has its own meeting. Players hunker down to watch and analyze footage of the mistakes they made in yesterday's game.

2:00 p.m. Players hit the field to do "on-field corrections"—a walk-through practice without any gear—to fix the plays they botched in yesterday's game.

3:00 p.m. Call it quits for the day.

TUESDAY—A DAY OFF

Whew! Players kick back and rest their sore and football-weary bones.

WEDNESDAY—HUMP DAY

This middle-of-the-week day may be the toughest and longest day of practice but, once it's over, game day is a lot closer.

6:30 a.m. Players report for treatment of injuries. And if they're not on time, some teams may make them pay fines.

7:45 a.m. Players have a Special Teams meeting like the one on Monday. But the team quarterbacks have their own meeting.

8:30 a.m. The coach gives everyone the lowdown on the strengths and weaknesses of their next opponent. Players watch footage of the opposing team in action, get reports on individual players, and get the playbook for the week. Then the offensive and defensive players have their own meetings to study the playbook.

10:45 a.m. Players hit the field to walk through the plays they've just studied. Coaches show the upcoming opponent's plays on cue cards. Team scouts then line up in the opposing team's formations that players have just seen on film and in the playbook, so players can learn to recognize them on the field.

Players Hit the Books

At training camp, players receive a playbook of their team's secret plays and strategies. It may be as long as 800 pages, and players must know it inside out. What's more, every week the coaching staff writes a new 250 plus–page playbook for the upcoming game, with zillions of their opponent's plays, reports on players, and plays to counter the opponent's plays. That way, players will recognize the opponent's plays and know what to do in the heat of the action without having to stop and think. Who knew playing football required so much study?

11:10 a.m. Lunchtime! Players grab a bite and a break. The head coach, the quarterback, and star players may talk to news reporters.

12:00 p.m. It's back to the meeting rooms to review the plays.

12:30 p.m. Players go out to the practice field and do drills for running, handling the ball, and making hits. The team's video department films the whole practice.

2:30 p.m. Coaches and players watch footage of the day's two-hour practice to see what went right and wrong. That way, they can smooth out problems tomorrow.

4:30 p.m. The team packs it in for the day. But before they do, players will have squeezed in a workout lifting weights and running sprints. Whew!

THURSDAY—NOT AGAIN!

No, it's not a dream. Players pretty much repeat the same schedule as Wednesday. The only difference is that they study and practice different plays and parts of the game.

FRIDAY—DÉJÀ VU, TAKE TWO

Yup, Friday is another repeat of Wednesday. Coaches usually cut the practice short but not necessarily the meetings.

7:00 p.m. On a "short" day like this, the defensive players may get together for dinner at a teammate's or go out to eat. The offensive players do the same. It's a chance to hang out with their gang.

SATURDAY—COUNTDOWN TO GAME DAY

A.M. Players get treatment for injuries, go to meetings, and walk through plays again.

P.M. The team may meet again at the team hotel for a final review of the opponent. Players get psyched for Game Day tomorrow!

SUNDAY—GAME DAY

Players arrive at the stadium pumped and ready to rock. They get dressed to kill, er, play:

12:00 p.m. Teams head out to the field to warm up as fans stream into the stands. Then they return to the locker room briefly.

1:00 p.m. Teams take the field. The referee tosses a coin. The team that wins the coin toss chooses to kick or receive the ball. Then teams go head to head on the gridiron, trying to outwit, outsmart, outthink, outmuscle, outplay, and outdo each other in each and every way.

4:30 p.m. The final buzzer of the game sounds and it's all over. Whether they've won or lost, many players are banged up, cut, and bruised. If it's an away game, they board a plane and fly home.

In-flight Treatment of any obvious injuries begins on the plane. Trainers bandage up cuts and sprains and break out ice packs to reduce swelling of any lumps and bumps players took for the team.

Midnight Chances are some of the coaching staff are already preparing a battle plan for the next game, watching footage of the upcoming opponent's games to spot their strengths and weaknesses. And so the weekly grind begins again on the gridiron.

LEGENDS OF THE GAME

Bronko Nagurski
(with ball)

How the Giants Outsmarted the Bears

The Chicago Bears were on top of the world as they headed into the 1934 NFL championship game. The Bears had charged through the regular season with a perfect record—all wins and no losses. Whereas their opponents, the New York Giants, had fumbled through the season with eight wins and five losses.

The night before the big game, freezing rain fell on Polo Grounds, New York. The field froze, patches of ice formed, and neither team could get a firm footing the next day.

Even though the Giants had home field advantage, the Bears bounced ahead 10–3 by halftime. But the Giants weren't about to pack it in! When one of their players thought that basketball shoes would give them better grip, the coach dispatched equipment manager Abe Cohen to buy the shoes.

The only problem was that no stores were open. But Cohen was a man on a mission! According to NFL lore, Cohen broke into the lockers of Manhattan College with a hammer and "borrowed" their basketball shoes.

Whatever happened, Cohen returned with nine pairs of sneakers and the Giants laced them up for the second half. The soft-soled shoes gave the Giants better traction than the Bears. "We were slipping and sliding around and they were running all over us," former Bear Bronko Nagurski said years later.

The Giants leaped ahead 30–13. The sneakers seemed to give the Giants the winning edge, and the game became known as the "sneakers game." Later Nagurski declared, "They just outsmarted us."

Chapter 6

THE SCIENCE OF EXPLOSIVE MOVES

Whoosh! A quarterback lets a pass rip, a receiver leaps up to make the catch, and bolts over the goal line for a touchdown. *Boom!* A tackle hits a ball carrier and takes him down and out of the action. *Hut!* A center snaps the ball to a punter, opponents rush over the line of scrimmage to try to block the punt. *Whomp!* The punter boots the ball up, up, and away!

What makes passes, hits, and kicks so exciting and explosive beyond the effort players put into them? Find out exactly how these moves electrify the game and make fans jump out of their seats with a roar. *Woo hoo!*

Blast into Action!

PUNTING THE BALL

Today, many placekickers wear soccer shoes to kick the ball soccer-style with the inside edge of the foot rather than the toe. Sound crazy? Over the years, some kickers have kicked barefoot to get a better feel for the ball.

Okay, maybe punting the ball doesn't seem like an explosive move. After all, teams usually punt on a fourth down, giving up the ball when they're struggling to make the 10 yards needed for a new set of downs. But nothing changes the field position of the game like a punt. Check it out.

Ready, Set, Punt!

A punter sets up about 15 yards behind the line of scrimmage (LOS). A teammate lines up halfway between the punter and the LOS to block anyone who might break through to block the punt. The center snaps the ball and feeds it to the punter in less than a second flat. The punter catches it, takes one or two steps, and drops the ball to kick it. *Boom!*

Getting Hang Time

The greater the vertical distance the ball travels, the longer it hangs in the air. NFL punters aim for a hang time of 4.5 seconds. A kick that sends the ball spinning in a spiral can make the ball hang in the air longer and fly faster and farther than a kick that sends the ball tumbling end over end.

No Easy Job

A punter has two goals. One: to kick the ball as far away from his end zone as possible so his opponents are less likely to score on the return. Two: to make the ball hang in the air as long as possible so his teammates have time to hotfoot it downfield and tackle the kick returner, who's trying to catch the ball and run it back.

Playing, er, Punting the Angles

The angle of the kick helps determine the hang time and how far the ball travels over the field. A steep angle (60°) sends the ball high up for a long hang time and a relatively short distance away from the LOS. A shallow angle (30°) results in less hang time but makes the ball travel a longer distance away from the LOS.

Arcing Over the Field

Whenever a football sails through the air, it cuts a curved path due to the force of gravity. As the force of a kick or pass sends the ball up, the force of gravity pulls it down to Earth.

60°

30°

Veritcal Distance

Getting Distance

The greater the horizontal distance the ball travels, the farther the ball moves away from the punter's end zone. NFL punters try to boot the ball at least 45 yards beyond the LOS.

Horizontal Distance

Kicking vs. Punting

Just in case you were wondering, kicking is not the same as punting. In fact, teams usually have different players for each and some even have another player for kickoffs. Here's the scoop:

Play	Who	When	Where	Tee Used?	Destination
Kickoff	Placekicker or kickoff specialist	Opening of game, beginning of second half, after every score	Team's 30-yard line	Yes	Downfield away from end zone
Field goal attempts	Placekicker	Up to coach's discretion when team has possession	7 yards behind LOS	No, a player holds the ball in place	Over the crossbar between the goal-post's uprights
Extra point attempts	Placekicker	After scoring a touchdown	7 yards behind LOS	No, a player holds the ball in place	Over the crossbar between the goal-post's uprights
Punt	Punter	On a fourth down	15 yards behind LOS	No, the punter receives the snap and drops the ball to kick it	Downfield away from end zone

STAR

Tom Dempsey was an exceptional kicker like no other. Dempsey was born with the toes of his right foot missing, and his unusual foot proved to be perfect for kicking. In 1970, Dempsey hammered the ball with it for a record-setting 63-yard field goal.

Tom Dempsey

Why punt on a fourth down instead of going for the yards?

It comes down to field position. Unless a team is behind their opponent's 40-yard line, they don't want to risk not gaining the yards and giving up the ball to their opponents within easy scoring reach of their own end zone. They'd rather boot the ball to send their opponents as far away from their end zone as possible.

Can a punt returner get a touchdown?

Yes, and how! Sometimes a punt returner can rip and zip down the field through an opponent's entire lineup all the way to the end zone, rocking the ball for a touchdown.

What if a punt returner "muffs a kick"?

When a punt returner fails to get the ball, the punting team may pounce on it but they cannot advance it on the play. But if the returner touches the ball and fumbles it, the ball is up for grabs.

TACKLING THE BIG HIT

Wham! Bam! Gotcha, Sam! A linebacker tackles a ball carrier, knocks the ball out of his hands, and slams him to the turf. When players tackle, they use their hands and arms to bring down the player who has the ball. What packs the punch of these big hits? Check out the forces at work in a tackle and see.

MAY THE FORCE BE EQUAL

When any two players collide—whether each is big or small, or fast or slow—the forces they exert on each other are equal and opposite in direction. Those are the laws of motion. So why does a smaller player often go flying through the air? A smaller player has less mass than a bigger one. Therefore, he also weighs less. So the force of gravity that attracts him, and all objects, to the Earth is smaller.

CENTER OF WHAT?

All objects are made of matter. A player's mass is the amount of matter in his body. His center of mass is the point where his mass is greatest. (In guys, this is above the belly button. In gals, it is below the belly button.) When a force like a hit strikes the player on either side of his center of mass, the player will rotate around this center. So if he's upright, he may go down. *Slam!*

THE TRUTH BEHIND THE INCREDIBLE BULK

No doubt about it. Some players, like offensive tackle Willie Anderson (see right), are massive. In fact, at the beginning of training camp for the 2006 NFL season, more than five hundred players weighed in over 135 kg (300 lbs.). Offensive tackles like Anderson are the biggest players in the game, because their job is to protect the quarterback by staying between him and the defensive linemen who are gunning for him. The more a player weighs, the bigger his mass. And mass matters. According to the laws of motion that govern our universe, the more massive a player (or any object), the more his body will want to continue doing whatever it's doing—moving or staying still. So the less likely he is to be stopped, shoved aside, slowed down, or knocked down by an outside force—a.k.a. a hit from another player. Is it any wonder that so many players are so massive in the hard-hitting game of football?

HIT LOW TO DELIVER A BLOW

Effective linemen know to tackle ball carriers down low. When a lineman hits a ball carrier low (above, left) rather than high (above, right), he strikes the carrier farther away from the carrier's center of mass. And the farther he strikes from the center of mass, the less force he needs to make the carrier rotate around the center of mass and go down. Of course, linemen don't study physics to know this. They learn it on the gridiron's "school of hard hits."

STAR ★ ••••••••••••••••••••

T.O. is no easy foe to tackle. The star wide receiver, a.k.a. Terrell Owens, has the size, strength, and speed to dance his way through the clutches of a team's entire lineup of defenders. When T.O. gets the ball, you better "getcha popcorn ready." In three seasons, he averaged a touchdown per game. What's more, T.O. danced all over the opponents' end zones to celebrate and rub it in.

Terrell Owens

THE BULLET PASS

Players and TV announcers don't call an awesome pass a "bullet pass" for nothing. A well-thrown short pass really does fly through the air like a bullet. Check it out and see it spin.

TIP

If a quarterback stands a few yards behind the center and receives the ball in-flight—a.k.a. a shotgun snap—watch for the next play to be a pass rather than a run. Getting the ball in the shotgun position means the quarterback doesn't have to drop back. He can scan the field and target his receivers better.

Firing a Pass

A football has an oblong shape like a bullet. To throw a pass, a quarterback raises the ball in his hand slightly above and behind his head. Then he brings his arm forward rapidly and releases the ball. As he lets the ball go, he snaps his wrist down and out to give the ball spin.

Spinning Like a Bullet

The spin the quarterback gives the ball makes the ball turn in a tight spiral just like a speeding bullet. (When a rifle fires, spiral grooves inside the barrel give a bullet spin.) This spiral spin keeps the ball flying straight through the air nose-first without tumbling or wobbling. That way it can meet its target—the hands of a receiver.

A Nose for Speed

Whizzing through the air nose-first like a bullet rather than belly-first also cuts down on air drag, or resistance, met by the ball as it bumps into air molecules, the microscopic clumps of atoms that make up air. That's because a smaller area of the ball strikes the air molecules. The result? A nose-first pass travels faster than a belly-first pass.

STAR

In the 1970s, quarterback Terry Bradshaw led the Pittsburgh Steelers to four Super Bowl wins. The strong-armed quarterback had an unusual way of throwing passes. As Bradshaw gripped the ball, he placed his index finger on the back tip.

This added more force to his throws, increasing the speed of his passes, and gave the ball more spin, increasing its steadiness in the air. How's that for having a finger on the pulse?

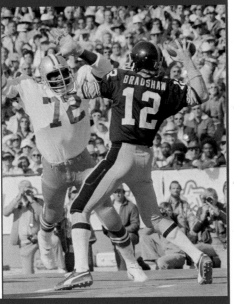

Terry Bradshaw

What's the bomb?

When the bomb goes off, look out. Not only is it one of football's most exciting plays but it's also one of the most bungled. The bomb is a long pass that fires the ball 40 yards or more into the ready and waiting hands of a receiver.

What makes a pass complete?

Catching the ball. No joke! In football speak, a forward pass caught by a receiver inbounds is called a completion.

How fast is a pass?

Star quarterbacks like Peyton Manning (below) throw some of the fastest passes in the NFL, which clock in at speeds of more than 65 km (40 mi.) per hour.

TRY THIS!

Quick Hit

A strong-armed quarterback can hurl the ball as far as 80 yards. *Whoosh!*

How does spin affect the flight of the ball? Try this experiment and see.

YOU WILL NEED

- a football

1 Throw the football without any spin. Hold the ball in your hand. Then just push the ball forward and release it. What happens?

2 Throw the ball with spin. Place your middle finger on the third lace from the end of the ball and the inside of your little finger on the fifth lace to get a good grip. Push the ball forward and, as you release it, snap your wrist down and out to give the ball spin. What happens?

Answer on page 64.

Bradbury Robinson

The Ball Takes Flight

Coach Eddie Cochems was fed up. His team, St. Louis University, was getting nowhere trying to run the ball in a game against Carroll College. So the coach ordered his players to break out the "air attack."

That was the situation in Waukesha, Wisconsin, in September 1906. Back then, teams didn't throw the ball much because the forward pass had just become legal. But the rule change had prompted Coach Cochems to study the ball.

Once Cochems discovered that the ball's laces give players' fingers something to grip onto to throw it, he focused the entire training camp on passing. Cochems told his players to put their fingers between the laces of the ball and throw it with a "twist of the wrist" to make it spiral through the air.

The result thrilled Bradbury Robinson: "Coach, I can throw the dang thing 40 yards!" After that the team secretly practiced forward passes but had yet to try one in a game. So Robinson launched the air attack with a pass to Jack Schneider. The bold move caught the Carroll defense off guard, but the pass was incomplete and St. Louis had to give up the ball.

That didn't stop the air attack, though. When St. Louis got the ball back, Robinson fired to Schneider again. Schneider caught the ball this time and zoomed over the Caroll goal line for a touchdown. St. Louis trounced Carroll 22–0. What's more, the team went on to use the air attack to win each and every game that year.

Chapter 7

GAME TIME

We're here to fight! We'll win this game tonight! We're here to move. Get in the groove!" That's what some cheerleaders chant to set the tone for victory. But no matter what cheerleaders, fans, and players chant and cheer, excitement crackles in the air as soon as the players burst out of the tunnel from the locker room to the field.

The team captains meet the referee at center field. The referee tosses a coin and the visiting captain gets to call heads or tails. The winner of the coin toss then decides whether to receive the ball or to defend a particular end zone. If the winner chooses the ball, the other captain gets the pick of end zones. And with that, one team kicks the ball to the other—*whomp!*—and the battle is underway. Get the skinny on game time action and how teams vie for a winning edge.

Louisiana State
University (LSU) Tigers

Get Your
Front Row Seat

BATTLE STATIONS

As players take their places on the field, the coaching staff hunker down at their battle stations—the bench and the booth. They use surveillance and communication equipment to collect "enemy intelligence" and feed it to the players. Check it out!

UP, UP, IN THE BOOTH

The defensive coordinator and assistant coaches usually stake out the booth in the press box at the top of the stadium. This gives them a bird's eye view of the game action unfolding below, allowing them to recognize the opponents' formations and identify offensive and defensive strategies. They look for little things that can give the team an edge. For example, they might notice that an opposing linebacker takes a certain stance when the defense is about to blitz. They communicate all this information through headsets to the head coach and other coaching staff at the bench, who then pass on the nitty-gritty to the players at large. Sometimes, they also talk to specific players one-on-one over the phone. *Brrrring! Brrrring!* Coach calling, booth to bench.

THE BENCH

Looking for the head coach and offensive coordinator on the sidelines? They're the dudes yammering away on headsets, talking to the coaching staff in the booth and the quarterback. Since all video equipment is off limits during the game, one of them has a printout of the game plan, which details the team's opening plays and formations, along with options for different field positions and situations. As the coaches in the booth feed them "enemy intelligence" and what's working and what isn't, the head coach communicates with the troops on the field. What's more, fax machines at the bench spit out photos taken by cameras perched around the stadium. The photos reveal the opponents' formations, player stances, and where each opponent moves on his first step. The coaches share this intelligence with the players, making any adjustments to win.

Spying Coach Busted!

It's no secret that coaches spend hours watching videotapes of opponents, trying to crack their codes by matching their signals to the actions that unfold. In fact, one coach routinely sent a scout out to watch opponents' signals firsthand. And some always cover their mouths as they call plays from the sidelines just in case their opponents are trying to read their lips. But that doesn't mean anything goes. In 2007, the NFL busted Bill Belichick, head coach of the New England Patriots, for spying on the New York Jets' defensive signals, when the team's video assistant was caught with a video camera on the Jets' sideline. The league fined Belichick and fined the team, and took away some of the team's draft picks. The fact is, NFL rules forbid teams from using video recording devices of any kind during games. And videotaping an opponent's signals is strictly forbidden. Case closed.

Game Changers

Meet some players who can change a game in seconds flat with one big play. In fact, opponents often design game plans to hold these guys at bay.

Running Back

LaDainian Tomlinson
No running back can change the game like L.T.—a.k.a. LaDainian Tomlinson (above right). L.T. moves through holes in the defense that no one else can even see, making extraordinary plays that can turn a game in an instant. In 2006, L.T. scored a record-setting thirty-one touchdowns.

Wide Receiver

Randy Moss
You just got "Mossed"! That's the saying around the NFL when wide receiver Randy Moss (above left) gets by a tackler and boots it with the ball all the way to the house. Moss's ability to elude opponents and spectacular one-handed catches make him a threat to change the game every time.

Return Specialist

Devin Hester
Left, right, left, right. *Zoom*—and he's gone! Devin Hester cuts his way around defenders, leaving them to eat his dust. The return specialist can turn a game around in a flash, returning a kick or a punt for a touchdown. Hester set a record for the most kick returns in a single season. Some fans call him "Anytime."

Free Safety

Ed Reed
Free safety Ed Reed likes to get his hands on the ball and has a knack for making interceptions that turn games around. Reed once returned an interception for a record-setting 108 yards! He is also an expert at tackling and forcing fumbles. He's ready to rumble anytime, anywhere.

ONLY IN FOOTBALL

Quick Hit

In 2010, six countries, including the U.S. and Canada, participated in the first women's world championship of football.

Where else could a running back and rookie foil an assassin? A two-minute drill change the outcome of an entire game? Or a player use "not-so-secret intelligence" to outwit opponents? Check out some sizzling action that has stunned football fans, players, and coaches alike.

FRENCHY, THE ASSASSIN, AND THE ROOKIE

In 1972, the Pittsburgh Steelers were down 7–6 to the Oakland Raiders on a fourth down, with only 26 seconds on the clock. Steelers' quarterback Terry Bradshaw sent up a pass to teammate John "Frenchy" Fuqua at the 35-yard line. But Frenchy wasn't alone. The Assassin—Raiders' safety Jack Tatum—homed in on the incoming ball, too. And he rammed into Frenchy as the pass arrived. Frenchy and the ball went flying. Mission accomplished! The only thing was that Pittsburgh rookie running back Franco Harris scooped up the ball and ran it all the way to the end zone for a touchdown. "Tell them you touched it, Frenchy!" The Assassin demanded. According to the rules back then, once an offensive player touched the ball, no other offensive player could touch it unless a defensive player touched it first. So if the ball had touched Frenchy without touching The Assassin, the rookie's touchdown was illegal. The officials scratched their heads, but finally let the touchdown stand. And to this day, Frenchy has never confessed whether he touched the ball.

JOHNNY U'S TWO-MINUTE DRILL

At the 1958 NFL Championship Game, the New York Giants led the Baltimore Colts 17–14 with just two minutes to go, when Colts' quarterback Johnny Unitas fired up the field with a "two-minute drill." Calling plays with the briskness of a drill sergeant, Unitas spearheaded a drive of short, quick passes to receiver Raymond Berry. Johnny U's drill marched the Colts downfield within range of a field goal and, with just seven seconds left, the Colts' kicker tied the game. *Bzzzzzt.* The final buzzer went and the Colts and the Giants found themselves in sudden-death overtime. The first team to score would win. Johnny U took charge again, driving the Colts 80 yards downfield. Unitas hit Berry with a pass at the 1-yard line. Then just when the Giants were convinced that he was going to pass again, Unitas handed the ball to fullback Alan "The Horse" Ameche, who galloped into the end zone. Touchdown, Colts! Fans cheered and Johnny U's two-minute drill became a standard mode of attack in close games.

WIN AT ANY COST

10, 9, 8... The last seconds of the game were ticking down, and quarterback Ken "The Snake" Stabler (above) was running out of options at the 14-yard line. His team, the 1978 Oakland Raiders, was behind, 20–14, to the San Diego Chargers. The Snake wound up to pass, but saw he was about to get sacked. So he deliberately fumbled the ball forward. The ball rolled to the 12-yard line, where running back Pete Banaszak managed to bat it forward. Tight end Dave Casper got to it next, kicked it into the end zone, and then fell on the ball to tie the game. *Oof!* The Chargers protested, but the ref ruled that the touchdown was legal. Then kicker Errol Mann put the Chargers away by getting an extra point. The next season, the NFL made it illegal to advance the ball downfield by swatting or kicking it. Nevertheless, the Raiders stood by the play. "The play is in our playbook," Oakland guard Gene Upshaw once said. "It's called 'Win at Any Cost.'"

CORNERBACK JUMPS A RUNNING ROUTE

Sometimes, defensive players can turn the tables on their opponents and score big. Take Super Bowl XLIV in 2010: late in the fourth quarter, New Orleans Saints' cornerback Tracy Porter (far right) spotted Indianapolis Colts' wide receiver Austin Collie (near right) going into motion at the line of scrimmage and recognized the Colts' formation. Then, thanks to all the footage of the Colts he had studied to prepare for the big game, Porter knew that Colts quarterback Peyton Manning would try to hit receiver Reggie Wayne with a pass long enough to get a first down. Porter used this not-so-secret intelligence and jumped onto Wayne's running route, intercepting the pass. Once he had the ball, Porter sprinted 74 yards for a touchdown. The play sealed the game, and the Saints marched on to victory, 31–17.

STAR ★ • • • • • • • • • • • • • • • • • •

New York Jets' quarterback Joe Namath, a.k.a. Broadway Joe, had a natural showmanship that attracted the spotlight. In 1968, when the Jets were about to meet the heavily favored Baltimore Colts in the Super Bowl, Namath made a personal guarantee his team would win. People thought it was just big talk. But Namath backed it up with a rock-solid performance, passing for 206 yards and fueling the Jets to upset the Colts, 16–7.

Joe Namath

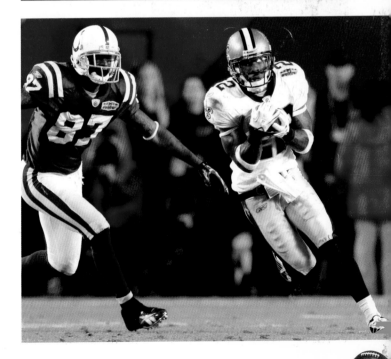

LINE UP IN FORMATION

Football is a bit like a supersize game of chess. Teams line up their players on the gridiron in formations, or arrangements, for particular plays. Get the skinny on the offensive and defensive formations you're likely to see in the football nation.

For a refresher on who's who and what these positions do, see page 14.

OFFENSIVE FORMATIONS

The "T" Formation

If you play football, chances are you've seen your opponents line up in this T-shaped formation. Or maybe your own team uses it on plays to run the ball. Notice how it has three running backs lined up in a row behind the quarterback. This is the oldest formation in the football nation. As teams began to pass the ball more, it fell out of use among the pros.

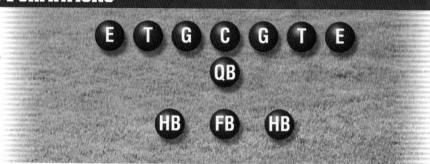

The Pro "T" or Split "T" Formation

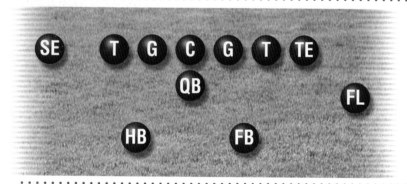

As pro teams bumped up the passing game, splitting the "T" formation gave them an extra wide receiver, the flanker, along with the split end and tight end for three receivers in all. With two running backs split, or positioned on opposite sides of the quarterback, this formation allows teams to run or pass the ball to either side of the field. So the defense has a tough time telling what the offense is going to do. Maybe that's why this is one of the pros' most popular offensive formations today.

The "I" Formation

Teams can run or pass from this formation in which a fullback and a tailback line up behind the quarterback in the shape of the letter "I." The fullback usually blocks for the tailback who carries the ball. The formation allows the tailback to hit full stride by the time he reaches the line of scrimmage. It also allows the tailback to see where his blockers are, see how the defense responds to the play, and spot holes in the defense to skedaddle through. Maybe it should be called "I Spy"!

Chess on the Gridiron

- A team chooses offensive formations that help their players do whatever they do best—run or pass the ball.

- When an offense takes a particular formation, they watch and wait to see how the defense lines up. Then if the defense lines up the same way the next time they take that formation, they have discovered a "characteristic" of the defense that they can try to use to their advantage.

- For example, once the offense knows what the defense is likely to do, they can adjust their play to break through any "soft spots" they see in the defense.

- The T formation has three running backs. Other formations have fewer running backs and more receivers. The fewer the running backs, the lesser the threat of the team's running attack and the greater the threat of its passing attack. Defenses know this and can adjust their coverage accordingly.

- What teams learn about their opponents in the first quarter helps them choose what formations and plays to run in the rest of the game.

DEFENSIVE FORMATIONS

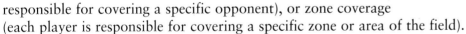

The 4–3 Front

Today, most NFL teams use this defensive formation named for the number of linemen and linebackers, 4 and 3, in it. The 4–3 front can stop both the pass and the run. It also allows defenders to use man-to-man coverage (each player is responsible for covering a specific opponent), or zone coverage (each player is responsible for covering a specific zone or area of the field).

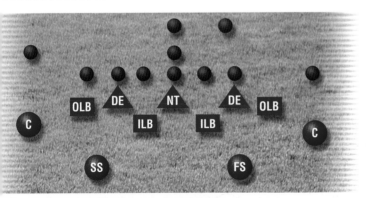

The 3–4 Front

No one defensive formation can cover all situations. So teams switch up as needed. The 3–4 front has three linemen and 4 linebackers up front and is more effective at stopping the pass than the 4–3 front. The extra linebacker can drop back to help cover passes and also run at the quarterback.

Defensive Positions

C	=	Cornerback
DE	=	Defensive End
DT	=	Defensive Tackle
FS	=	Free Safety
ILB	=	Inside Linebacker
MLB	=	Middle Linebacker
NT	=	Nose Tackle
OLB	=	Outside Linebacker
SS	=	Strong Safety

RULES & REGS

THE FIELD

Football is played on a field shaped like a rectangle so play can flow between two end zones.

Sideline When the ball and/or a player go beyond the sideline, they are out of bounds.

50-yard line This line runs down the middle of the field, dividing the field in half.

End line The line at each end of the field.

End zone The scoring zone—an area 10 yards long between the goal line and end line.

Goal post The post that stands at the center of the end line.

Goal line The goal line represents an imaginary wall, or plane, on the field. To score, a player has only to break the plane of the goal line with the ball.

Field numbers and yard lines On an NFL field, yard lines appear every 5 yards and field numbers every 10 yards to help players and fans tell how far a team has to move the ball for a first down.

Arrows A white arrow pointing toward the nearest end zone appears at every number except that for the 50-yard line.

Chain crew or gang A group of three people: two rodmen who use a 10-yard-long chain attached to two rods to measure distances critical for first downs when called for by officials; and a boxman who holds a marker that shows where the ball is and which down it is.

Officials In the NFL, a group of seven officials oversees and enforces the rules of the game.

Team bench Each team has its own bench about 12 feet behind the sideline. Players, coaches, team doctors, and trainers hang out in this area during games.

Hash marks White marks appear one yard apart to help officials spot the ball. All plays begin in the area between the two center sets of hash marks.

Goal post To score a field goal or an extra point after a touchdown, teams must kick the ball over the crossbar and between the two uprights of the goal post.

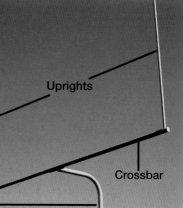

Uprights

Crossbar

NFL vs. CFL

Football is football, right? Nope. The rules of the game just aren't the same in the NFL and CFL. Check out the key differences:

- NFL teams have four downs, or chances, to make 10 yards whereas CFL teams have only three.

- NFL fields are 10 yards shorter and about 12 yards narrower than CFL fields.

- In the NFL, the goalposts stand on the end line but, in the CFL, they stand on the goal line.

- NFL teams play with eleven players apiece on the field while CFL teams play with twelve. This extra player takes a backfield position and results in different formations.

- NFL teams have a tight end, a player who lines up with the offensive linemen at the line of scrimmage. CFL teams often have a slotback, a player who is a large receiver like a tight end but can also do the job of a running back. The slotback lines up in the slot—the area between the offensive line and wide receiver (see right).

- In the NFL, offensive and defensive linemen set up "eyeball to eyeball" at the line of scrimmage—with only the length of the ball to separate them. In the CFL, defensive linemen set up one full yard away from the line of scrimmage.

- In the NFL, once players set up at the line of scrimmage, only one offensive player can move before the snap. However, in the CFL, every offensive player in the backfield is free to move except the quarterback.

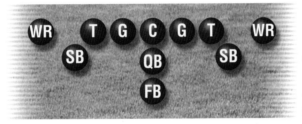

- In the NFL, receivers need to have both feet in bounds for a catch to count as a reception but, in the CFL, receivers need only one foot in bounds.

- NFL punt returners can wave an arm in the air to signal a fair catch. This means opponents must let the returner catch the ball without interference and he cannot try to advance the ball downfield. No such fair catch rule exists in the CFL.

- In the CFL, a team can score a single point, called a rouge, on a kick or a punt if the ball goes into the end zone and the opponent doesn't return it out of the end zone, or if the ball sails through the end zone. In the NFL, no such scoring opportunities exist.

- Even the ball is different (see page 11).

The slotback (SB) lines up in the slot between the wide receiver (WR) and offensive linemen.

HOW TO PLAY

- The object of the game is to score points by moving the ball into the opponent's end zone.

- The team who scores the most points wins.

- In the NFL, each team may have no more than eleven players on the field at once. The team with the ball is on offense and the team without the ball is on defense.

- In the NFL, the team on offense has four downs—plays or chances—to move the ball 10 yards downfield. If they do not gain 10 yards, they must give up the ball.

HOW TO SCORE

There are five different ways to score points in football. Teams can score:

- 6 points for a touchdown by getting the ball into the other team's end zone.

- 1 point for an extra point after a touchdown by kicking the ball over the crossbar and between the uprights of the goal post.

- 2 points for a two-point conversion after a touchdown by getting the ball into the other team's end zone again.

- 3 points for a field goal by kicking the ball over the crossbar and between the uprights of the goal post.

- 2 points for a safety by tackling an opponent who has the ball in his own end zone or getting an opponent to take a penalty in his end zone. This allows teams to score points while on defense. Not only do they get the points, but they also get the ball!

Air-it-out football — passing the ball on most plays.

Audible — codes called by the quarterback, at the line of scrimmage, to change the play.

Blitz — when more than five defensive players rush or run at the quarterback.

Block — making contact with an opponent using your hands, arms, and shoulders to move the opponent aside.

Bomb — a long pass.

Breaking the plane — when the ball breaks an imaginary wall, or plane, at the goal line to score.

Bullet pass — a well-thrown short pass.

Center — an offensive linemen who snaps the ball between his legs to the quarterback and calls signals for the line.

CFL — Canadian Football League.

Clear it out — when a wide receiver runs downfield luring defensive players on his tail to clear out an area for a shorter pass or running play.

Cleats — plastic, screw-in spikes or studs on the soles of players' shoes; also a term for shoes with cleats.

Completion — a forward pass caught inbounds by a receiver.

Conditioning — physical training.

Cornerback — a defensive player who lines up at a "corner" of a formation, usually opposite a wide receiver.

Defensive line — three or four defensive linemen who line up at the line of scrimmage.

Down — a period of play in which the offense tries to advance the ball.

End zone — the area at each end of the field where teams score by crossing the goal line with the ball.

Extra point — when a team scores a point after a touchdown by kicking the ball from the 2-yard line over the crossbar of the goal post between the uprights.

Fair catch — when a punt returner signals a catch by raising an arm in the air and waving it; then he can't run with the ball and players trying to tackle him can't touch him.

Field goal — when a team scores three points by kicking the ball from anywhere on the field over the crossbar of the goal post between the uprights.

First down — every time a team gets possession of the ball, it begins a first down; to get another first down, it must advance the ball at least 10 yards in four downs, or plays.

Formation — the way a team lines up for a particular play.

Free safety — a defensive player who lines up deep behind the middle linebacker to prevent big passing and running plays.

Fullback — a running back who often blocks or clears the way for a halfback who is carrying the ball.

Fumble — when an offensive player loses the ball by dropping it or by the force of a tackle.

Grey Cup — championship game of the CFL.

Guard — an offensive lineman who lines up next to the center.

Hail Mary — a pass thrown in desperation far away from the end zone.

Halfback — a running back who carries the ball, often following a fullback who clears the way.

Handoff — giving the ball to another player.

Hang time — length of time a ball is in the air during a punt or pass.

Huddle — when a team's players crowd together on the field to discuss the next play.

Incompletion — a forward pass that falls to the ground, is dropped by a receiver, or caught out of bounds.

Interception — a pass caught by an opponent.

Kickoff — kick that puts the ball into play at the start of the game and the third quarter as well as after every touchdown and field goal.

Line of scrimmage — where the ball sits on the field at the start of a play.

Linebacker — a defensive player who lines up behind the linemen.

Linemen — offensive and defensive players who line up at the line of scrimmage at the start of a play.

Man-to-man coverage — a style of defense in which each defender covers a specific offensive player.

Mental toughness — ability to deliver your best performance regardless of the competitive circumstances.

Middle linebacker — the "quarterback of the defense" who lines up behind the linemen and calls plays for the defense.

Neutral zone — the area between the offensive and defensive linemen at the line of scrimmage.

NFL — National Football League.

Nose tackle — a defensive player who lines up nose to nose with the center of the offensive line.

Offensive line — Five offensive linemen—a center flanked by two guards and two tackles outside the guards—who line up at the line of scrimmage.

Pass — when a player, usually the quarterback, throws the ball.

Pocket — an area the offensive line protects so the quarterback can pass the ball; the pocket extends 2 yards out from either offensive tackle and extends behind the offensive line to the team's end line and includes the tight end if he drops back to pass protect.

Point after touchdown (PAT) — see extra point.

Punt — when a player drops the ball and kicks it, usually on a fourth down.

Punter — a player who receives the ball from the snapper to drop it and kick it.

Quarterback — the player who leads the team's offense, receiving the ball from the center at the start of each play and then passing, handing off, or running with the ball.

Running back — an offensive player who runs with the ball, such as a halfback, fullback, or tailback.

Sack — tackling the quarterback behind the line of scrimmage before he can pass.

Safety — when the defense scores 2 points by tackling an opponent who has the ball in his own end zone or getting an opponent to take a penalty in his end zone.

Secondary — four defensive backs, two cornerbacks and two safeties, who line up behind the linebackers.

Special teams — players who take the field for kickoffs, punts, kickoff and punt returns, field goals and extra point attempts, and blocking field goals and extra point attempts.

Split end — a wide receiver who lines up on the line of scrimmage on the opposite side from the tight end.

Smashmouth football — running the ball on most plays to grind down a defense.

Snap — when the center throws the ball to the quarterback, punter, or ball holder for a kick attempt.

Strong safety — a defensive player who lines up behind the linebackers on the same side as the tight end.

Strong side — the side of the offensive line where the tight end lines up.

Super Bowl — championship game of the NFL.

Tackle — using your hands and arms to bring down an offensive player who has the ball; also a position on the offensive and defensive lines.

Tight end — a big wide receiver who lines up next to one of the offensive tackles and adds blocking power to the offensive line.

Two-point conversion — scoring 2 points after a touchdown with a pass or run into the other team's end zone rather than an extra point attempt.

Touchdown — scoring 6 points by getting the ball in the other team's end zone.

Visualization — mentally rehearsing moves so you can do them instinctively and successfully in games.

Weak side — the side of the offensive line without the tight end.

Wide receiver — an offensive player who uses speed and quickness to elude the defense and catch the ball.

Zone coverage — a style of defense in which each defender covers a specific zone or area of the field.

INDEX

Ameche, Alan "The Horse" 56
Anderson, Willie 49
Australian Football League 11

ball 7–12
    history 10–11
    how its made 9
    K ball 9, 11
Baltimore Colts 56, 57
Banaszak, Pete 57
Belichick, Bill 54
Berry, Raymond 56
Bradshaw, Terry 51, 56
Brady, Tom 27
Brees, Drew 32, 36

Camp, Walter 10
Canadian Football League
    (CFL) 4, 5, 11, 17, 18, 61
Carlisle Indians 12
Carolina Panthers 35
Carroll College 52
Casper, Dave 57
Chicago Bears 20, 25, 44
Cleveland Browns 27
coach 40, 42, 43, 54, 55
Cochems, Eddie 52
Collie, Austin 57

Dallas Cowboys 9, 11, 28
defense 14, 19
Dempsey, Tom 47
Denver Broncos 22
Dillon, Charlie 12
Ditka, Mike 20

Flutie, Doug 17
Football Hall of Fame 25
Freeney, Dwight 30, 32
Fuqua, John "Frenchy" 56

gear 38–39
    helmet 38, 40, 41
Green Bay Packers 25, 28, 41
Grey Cup 41

Haines, Hinkey 41
Harris, Franco 56
Harvard University 6, 10, 12

Hayes, Lester 39
Heinz Field 27
Hester, Devin 55
Houston Astrodome 22
Houston Oilers 22

Indianapolis Colts 32, 57
injuries 32, 33, 40
    injury report 33

Johnson, Jimmie 12

kicking 46, 47

laws of motion 48, 49

Manhattan College 44
Mann, Errol 57
Manning, Peyton 51, 57
McGill University 6, 10
McMahon, Jim 20
Miami Dolphins 26
Minnesota Vikings 19
Moss, Randy 55

Nagurski, Bronko 44
Naismith, James 40
Namath, Joe 57
New England Patriots 26,
    27, 54
New Orleans Saints 36, 57
New York Giants 44, 55, 56
New York Jets 26, 54, 57
nutrition 31

Oakland Raiders 27, 56, 57
offense 14, 18
Owens, Terrell 49

passing 50–51
Perry, William 20
Pittsburgh Steelers 9, 19, 26,
    27, 51, 56
player size 30, 38, 39
plays 42, 43, 54, 55, 58, 59
    calling 16
    playbook 42, 43
Plunkett, Jim 22
Porter, Tracy 57

positions 14–15, 58–59
    quarterback 16–17, 40,
                50, 51, 58, 59
punting 46, 47

Reed, Ed 55
Rice, Jerry 35
Robinson, Bradbury 52
Romo, Tony 11
Rooney, Art 27
Rose Bowl 36
rules 10, 11, 25, 33, 38, 39,
    52, 54, 56, 60–61

St. Louis University 52
San Diego Chargers 57
San Francisco 49ers 25
Saskatchewan Rough
    Riders 41
Schneider, Jack 52
Seattle Seahawks 22
Shula, Don 26
Smith, Emmitt 41
Smith, John 26
soccer 11
Stabler, Ken "The Snake" 56
Starr, Bart 28
steroids 33
strategy 14, 15, 18, 19, 54,
    55, 58, 59
Super Bowl 9, 20, 23, 27, 32,
    36, 51, 57

tackling 48–49
Tatum, Jack 56
Toma, George 25
Tomlinson, LaDainian 55
training 30, 42–43
    mental 34–35
turf 21–28
    Astroturf 22, 23
    FieldTurf 23

Unitas, Johnny 56
Upshaw, Gene 57

Warner, Kurt 32
Washington Redskins 19
Wayne, Reggie 57
Williams, DeAngelo 35
women 8, 56

Photo Credits

Roger Yip: Front cover, 3, 5 (girl), 17, 29, 30, 38, 39, 45, 50, 63; Brian Snyder/Reuters: 4, 30 (Colts), 59 (Porter); Jeff Haynes/Reuters: 5 (Bears), 36; Bettmann/CORBIS: 6, 44, 47, 51 (Bradshaw), 58; Wilson Sporting Goods: 9, 11 (Wilson Ball); World-rugby-museum.com: 10 (Ball); Robert Sorbo/Reuters: 11; Cumberland County Historical Society: 12; Jason Cohn/Reuters: 13; Str Old/Reuters: 17; Allen Fredrickson/Reuters: 18, 19; Berstein Associates/Getty Images: 20; Reuters Photographer/Reuters: 23; Stephen Dunn/Getty Images: 25; AP Photo/Mike Kullen: 26 (Snow Job); Andy Hayt /Sports Illustrated/Getty Images: 26 (Dolphins); Michael Fabus/Getty Images: 27 (Heinz Field); Gary Wiepert/Reuters: 27 (Brady); Vernon Biever/Getty Images: 28; Mike Segar/Reuters: 32 (Freeney); Reuter Photographer/Reuters: 32; Pierre Ducharme/Reuters: 35; Lucas Jackson/Reuters: 37; Jayne Oncea/Icon SMI: 39 (Hayes); Mark Wonderlin, courtesy of Schutt Sports: 40 (orange helmet), 41 (inside helmet); Ray Stubblebine/Reuters: 41 (Smith); Hulton-Deutsch Collection/CORBIS: 41 (full-face helmet); Jeff Haynes/Reuters: 43; Scott Boehm/Getty Images: 49 (Anderson); Mike Stone/Reuters: 49 (Owens); Matt Sullivan/Reuters: 51 (Manning); Jessica Rinaldi/Reuters: 53; Mike Blake/Reuters: 57 (Tomlinson); Adam Hunger/Reuters: 57 (Moss); Rebecca Cook/Reuters: 57 (Hester); Scott Audette/Reuters: 57 (Reed); Michael Zagaris/Getty Images: 59 (Stabler); Walter Iooss Jr./Sports Illustrated/Getty Images: 59 (Namath); All other images: Royalty-free (iStockphoto, Dreamstime)

Answers

Try This, page 35: Smiling on the outside when you feel nervous or scared on the inside is part of what's called "outside-in training." You do something on the outside—in the way you present yourself, act, or behave—that your brain and body interpret as feeling good and this makes you feel good inside. Smiling, for example, releases chemicals in your brain that trigger relaxation and feelings of happiness. In fact, smiling is one of the best "outside-in" things any player can do.

Try This, page 51: Throws without spin tend to send the ball tumbling through the air end over end on a crooked path. Whereas, throws with spin can send the ball nose-first through the air and keep it stable as it flies. This helps the ball travel on a straight path horizontally, and travel farther and faster than a throw without spin. What's more, this gives your throw more accuracy and makes it easier to catch.